Party Food & Appetizers

Everyday Cookery

STAR FIRE

This is a Starfire book
First published in 2005

05 07 09 08 06

1 3 5 7 9 10 8 6 4 2

Starfire is part of
The Foundry Creative Media Company Limited
Crabtree Hall, Crabtree Lane, Fulham, London, SW6 6TY

Visit our website: www.star-fire.co.uk

Copyright © The Foundry 2005

ISBN: 1-84451-309-2

The CIP record for this book is available from the British Library.

Printed in China

ACKNOWLEDGEMENTS

Publisher and Creative Director: Nick Wells
Project Editor and Editorial: Sarah Goulding
Design and Production: Chris Herbert, Mike Spender, Colin Rudderham and Claire Walker

Authors: Catherine Atkinson, Juliet Barker, Gina Steer, Vicki Smallwood,
Carol Tennant, Mari Mererid Williams, Elizabeth Wolf-Cohen and Simone Wright
Editorial: Gina Steer and Karen Fitzpatrick
Photography: Colin Bowling, Paul Forrester and Stephen Brayne
Home Economists and Stylists: Jacqueline Bellefontaine,
Mandy Phipps, Vicki Smallwood and Penny Stephens
Design Team: Helen Courtney, Jennifer Bishop, Lucy Bradbury and Chris Herbert

All props supplied by Barbara Stewart at Surfaces

NOTE
Recipes using uncooked eggs should be avoided by infants,
the elderly, pregnant women and anyone suffering from an illness.

Contents

Appetizers

Fish & Seafood

Meat

Poultry

Vegetables & Salads

Baking

Party Food

Meat

Poultry & Game

Vegetables & Salads

Puddings, Cakes & Baking

Entitaining

There are many ways of entertaining friends and family, and whether it's an informal or formal occasion, there are some rules that can be applied to all entertaining that will help make life easy for the host and hostess.

First of all, decide what kind of entertaining you wish to do: dinner party, supper, barbecue, picnic, cheese and wine or even a disco. This will dictate how formal the event will be, These days parties tend to be far more informal and relaxed, but even so it is still advisable to be guided by a few rules.

Make Life Easy

- Decide how many guests to invite and check their dietary requirements – are they vegetarian, do they have allergies to certain foods or have specific likes or dislikes?
- Choose the venue and menu and decide on the drinks to serve, ensuring that there are plenty of soft drinks for those driving.
- Make a shopping list ahead of time. This will allow for non-perishable foods to be bought early, as well as leaving time for a change of menu if necessary.
- Check china, cutlery, glasses and table linen. Make sure that it is clean and you have sufficient for all the guests.
- If it helps, work out a time plan early on. This will enable you to cook ahead if possible, thus saving time and effort on the day.
- If trying a new recipe, it is advisable to cook it beforehand to ensure that it works and tastes good.
- Arrange flowers the day before. Ensure you have nibbles and appetisers to serve, and stock up on ice, mixer drinks, lemon and glasses. Make sure you have plenty of coffee, tea or other after-dinner drinks.

Menu Planning for Different Occasions

Drinks Parties

These are normally semi-informal, and unless you serve very expensive wines or champagne, relatively cheap. Although food is not served as at an actual meal, it is a good idea to serve some light starters. This will help to offset too much alcoholic drink. People tend to eat more than you might think and it is a good idea to offer at least four or five different snacks as well as the obligatory nuts, crisps and little biscuits. Try to offer at least two vegetarian choices.

Try serving bite-sized vol-au-vents, perhaps filled with peeled prawns in a flavoured mayonnaise or chicken and sweetcorn. Small squares of quiche are good, or try roasted peppers with blue cheese. Smoked salmon and asparagus rolls, in both white and brown bread, cocktail sausages on sticks with a sweet chilli dip and chicken satay on sticks with satay sauces are all fairly straightforward. Hand round either small napkins or plates so guests can take a few at a time and do not spill the food on themselves or your furniture.

Keep drinks simple – do not offer everything. People are quite happy with a limited choice, red or white wine and beer with plenty of soft drinks is perfectly acceptable, or in winter try a warming punch. Pimms in the summer is an ideal choice.

Formal Dinner Party

These take a little more planning, both in terms of which guests to invite and the food. When working out the invitations, ensure that all your guests will get on well together and that there is at least one thing they have in common. Always remember to check their dietary requirements. Dinner parties can consist of as many courses as wished. If offering more than three, ensure that all the courses compliment each other and that the portions are not too large. Invite guests to arrive at least 30 minutes before you hope to sit down – this allows for guests arriving late.

Menus should be balanced: normally the dinner should start with a soup or small appetiser, and fish can be served either as the main course or as a second course as a prelude to the meat or poultry . Cheese and dessert are served after the main course; it is a matter of personal preference which is served first.

Supper, Lunch or Brunch Parties

These are normally much more informal and spur-of-the-moment events. However, a little planning is an excellent idea so that the host or hostess does not spend the entire time dashing around, making both themselves and

the guests stressed trying to ensure that everyone enjoys the occasion.

Obviously, the menu will depend on the time of year and the ages of those involved. Younger people are more than happy with fast food such as pizza or baked chicken pieces, with plenty of crisps and oven baked chips or a large bowl of pasta.

Try a theme for your party such as Italian or Oriental. There are many excellent Chinese and pasta dishes in this book to choose from.

Barbecue Parties

In this county, because of the weather, barbecues have to be fairly impromptu, meaning that the food needs to be simple and adaptable. Depending on tastes, keep the food quick and easy to prepare – the best choices are steak, chicken pieces, small whole fish such as sardines, and sausages, all of which can be cooked whole or cut into cubes and skewered and marinated to make kebabs. These cook quickly and will be ready in a very short time. Serve plenty of salads and bread. If cooking chicken portions which still contain the bones, it is advisable to cook them in the oven first and finish them on the barbecue to ensure that the chicken is thoroughly cooked through.

When barbecuing, it is vital that the food is cooked properly – semi-cooked sausages and chicken are one of the main causes of stomach upsets. If using a barbecue that uses coal, light it in plenty of time (at least 20 minutes before required) to allow the coals to reach the correct temperature before commencing to cook. The coals should be white/grey in colour and coated in

ash, and the flames should have died down to give a good, steady heat.

Eating outside often sharpens the appetite, so along with the meats serve plenty of bread or potatoes with assorted salads. Coleslaw and rice and pasta salads all work well. Keep desserts and drinks simple: fresh fruit, ice cream or cheese with wine or beer to drink.

Children's Parties

The highlight of any child's year is their birthday party, and to avoid tears, a little planning is a good idea. Many companies now offer a complete service so that the children can participate in an activity, such as skating, football or swimming, then the birthday tea is provided and all that is expected of the parents is to take and collect. This is by far one of the easiest and least stressful ways to celebrate their day, but can be expensive.

If that is not for you, above all keep it simple, whether you hold the party at home or in a local hall. First, decide on a date and venue and how long the party will be. Send out the invitations in plenty of time, stating clearly what time it will finish – most important for your sanity. Enlist the help of at least two other adults who are used to dealing with tears and tantrums. Decide on a few games, depending on age, such as pass the parcel, pin the tail on the donkey, musical chairs or blind man's bluff. Clear away furniture and any breakable ornaments and ensure that no sharp objects are in easy reach of little fingers.

Serve the food in a separate room and keep it fairly plain. Too much rich food could result in a few children being ill. Go for simple sandwiches, small pieces of cheese with grapes, sausages, sausage rolls, crisps, fairy cakes and, of course, a birthday cake. Serve squash to drink.

Many parties finish with the guests being issued with a goody bag to take home. If you do this, keep it simple: a few sweets, a piece of birthday cake and two or three very small gifts is perfectly acceptable. There is no need to spend a lot on these.

Wines

There are many different and excellent wines to choose from: white, red or rosé, sweet, medium or dry coming from all parts of the world. When choosing wines for a special occasion there are few points to bear in mind.

- Work out how many bottles you require. Allow 5–6 glasses from each bottle of wine; for fortified wines, sherry, Madeira and port allow 12–16 glasses. Champagne also yields between 5–6 glasses.

- Choose wines that are of medium price. Cheap wines taste cheap and your guests will not be impressed; expensive wines, on the other hand, will most probably not be appreciated in the general chat and movement.

- White wine is best served chilled. Place in the refrigerator at least the day before. If space is short, arrange for some ice for the day, place in a wine bucket or any clean container and chill the wine in this.

- Red wine should be served at room temperature, so if stored in a cool place, bring into another room and allow to come to room temperature. Open about 1–2 hours before serving. There is no need to decant either white or red wine, but it does look good and also allows red wine to breathe more easily. For wine with a heavy sediment it is advisable to decant it.

- For the greatest appreciation, red wine glasses should be wide-necked, allowing the bouquet to be enjoyed. White wine glasses are narrow at the neck. All should have a stem so that the glasses can be swirled in order to release the fragrance.

Know Your Wine

France
Renowned for its fine wines, Champagnes and excellent table wines. The Appellations d'Origines Contrôlées (A.O.C.) is a system that signifies if a wine comes from a fine wine region. Indicating different grades of quality, these appellations go in stages from simple wines to prized wines such as Beaune, Chateau Neuf du Pape and Sancerre. Simple vins des tables are blended wines that generally offer excellent value for money

Germany
German wines have improved considerably over the last 40 years. Gone, in the main, are the sweet white wines and heavy, rough reds. In their place are delicate, crisp wines from the Moselle and Rhine using the Riesling grape, and others such as Traminer, Sylvaner and other varieties blended together. Hock is perhaps one of the most well-known wines and comes from the four main regions in the Rhine. There are many fine wines, which carry the name of the grape.

Italy
Most of the regions of Italy produce wine, as do Sardinia and Sicily. When buying Italian wines, look for D.O.C. on the label. They produce both white and red, perhaps the most well-known of which is Chianti. This wine comes from Tuscany and is a fruity and robust wine and goes well with all red meats and game. Other red wines include Barolo from Piedmont and Valpolicella from the Veneto region. There are other excellent red wines from the north made from the Cabernet, Pinot and Merlot grapes.

Italy also produces some excellent white wines, ranging from Soave, Verdicchio, Frascati and Pinot Grigio – all have their own distinct style ranging from very dry, light wine to a heavier, sweeter wine.

Spain
Although Spain is world-famous for sherry, it also produces some excellent wines. The best-known is probably Rioja, which is produced both as white and red. This wine is produced throughout the whole of Spain, with the red Rioja coming in two styles, one being drier than the other, and the white tending to be full-bodied and dry.

New World
There are now some serious contenders to 'Old World' wines coming from as far afield as Australia – known as a 'New World' wine producer. Australia, South Africa, Chile and California all produce excellent wines that seriously challenge the established wine-growers. Growers from these countries have taken on-board all the established guidelines and knowledge and have expanded it to produce wines that are every bit as good. When buying New World wine, apply the same guidelines as for the established wines.

Store Cupboard Essentials
Ingredients for a Healthy Lifestyle

With the increasing emphasis on the importance of cooking healthy meals for your family, modern lifestyles are naturally shifting towards lower-fat and cholesterol diets. Low-fat cooking has often been associated with the idea that reducing fat reduces flavour, but this simply is not the case, which is great news for those trying to eat healthily. Thanks to the increasing number of lower-fat ingredients now available in shops, there is no need to compromise on the choice of foods we eat .

The store cupboard is a good place to start when cooking healthy meals. Most of us have fairly limited cooking and preparation time available during the week, and so choose to experiment during weekends. When time is of the essence, or friends arrive unannounced, it is a good idea to have some well thought-out basics in the cupboard, namely foods that are high on flavour whilst still being healthy.

As store cupboard ingredients keep reasonably well, it is worth making a trip to a good speciality grocery shop. Our society's growing interest in recent years with travel and food from around the world has led us to seek out alternative ingredients with which to experiment and incorporate into our cooking. Consequently, supermarket chains have had to broaden their product range and often have a specialist range of imported ingredients from around the world.

If the local grocers or supermarket only carries a limited choice of products, do not despair. The internet now offers freedom to food lovers. There are some fantastic food sites (both local and international) where food can be purchased and delivery arranged online.

When thinking about essentials, think of flavour, something that is going to add to a dish without increasing its fat content. It is worth spending a little bit more money on these products to make flavoursome dishes that will help stop the urge to snack on fatty foods.

Store Cupboard Hints

There are many different types of store cupboard ingredients readily available – including myriad varieties of rice and pasta – which can provide much of the carbohydrate required in our daily diets. Store the ingredients in a cool, dark place and remember to rotate them. The ingredients will be safe to use for six months.

Bulghur wheat A cracked wheat which is often used in tabbouleh. Bulghur wheat is a good source of complex carbohydrate.

Couscous Now available in instant form, couscous just needs to be covered with boiling water then forked. Couscous is a precooked wheat semolina. Traditional couscous needs to be steamed and is available from health food stores. This type of couscous contains more nutrients than the instant variety.

Dried fruit The ready-to-eat variety are particularly good as they are plump, juicy and do not need to be soaked. They are fantastic when puréed into a compote, added to water and heated to make a pie filling and when added to stuffing mixtures. They are also good cooked with meats, rice or couscous.

Flours A useful addition (particularly cornflour) which can be used to thicken sauces. It is worth mentioning that whole-grain flour should not be stored for too long at room temperature as the fats may turn rancid. While not strictly a flour, cornmeal is a very versatile low-fat ingredient which can be used when making dumplings and gnocchi.

Noodles Also very useful and can accompany any Far Eastern dish. They are low-fat and also available in the wholewheat variety. Rice noodles are available for those who have gluten-free diets and, like pasta noodles, provide slow-release energy to the body.

Pasta It is good to have a mixture of wholewheat and plain pasta as well as a wide variety of flavoured pastas. Whether fresh (it can also be frozen) or dried, pasta is a versatile ingredient with which to provide the body with slow-release energy. It comes in many different sizes and shapes; from the tiny tubettini (which can be added to soups to create a more substantial dish), to penne, fusilli, rigatoni and conchiglie, up to the larger cannelloni and lasagne sheets.

Pot and pearl barley Pot barley is the complete barley grain whereas pearl barley has the outer husk removed. A high cereal diet can help to prevent bowel disorders and diseases.

Pulses A vital ingredient for the store cupboard, pulses are easy to store, have a very high nutritional value and are great when added to soups, casseroles, curries and hot pots. Pulses also act as a thickener, whether flavoured or on their own. They come in two forms; either dried (in which case they generally need to be soaked overnight and then cooked before use – it is important to follow the instructions on the back of the packet), or canned, which is a convenient timesaver because the preparation of dried pulses can take a while. If buying canned pulses, try to buy the variety in water with no added salt or sugar. These simply need to be drained and rinsed before being added to a dish.

Kidney, borlotti, cannellini, butter and flageolet beans, split peas and lentils all make tasty additions to any dish. Baked beans are a favourite with everyone and many shops now stock the organic variety, which have no added salt or sugar but are sweetened with fruit juice instead.

When boiling previously dried pulses, remember that salt should not be added as this will make the skins tough and inedible. Puy lentils are a smaller variety. They often have mottled skins and are particularly good for cooking in slow dishes as they hold their shape and firm texture particularly well.

Rice Basmati and Thai fragrant rice are well suited to Thai and Indian curries, as the fine grains absorb the sauce and their delicate creaminess balances the pungency of the spices. Arborio is only one type of risotto rice – many are available depending on whether the risotto is meant to accompany meat, fish or vegetable dishes. When cooked, rice swells to create a substantial low-fat dish. Easy-cook American rice, both plain and whole-grain, is great for casseroles and for stuffing meat, fish and vegetables, as it holds its shape and firmness. Pudding rice can be used in a variety of ways to create an irresistible dessert.

Stock Good quality stock is a must in cooking as it provides a good flavour base for many dishes. Many supermarkets now carry a variety of fresh and organic stocks which although need refrigeration, are probably one of the most time- and effort-saving ingredients available. There is also a fairly large range of dried stock, perhaps the best being bouillon, a high-quality form of stock (available in powder or liquid form) which can be added to any dish whether it be a sauce, casserole, pie or soup.

Many people favour meals which can be prepared and cooked in 30–45 minutes, so helpful ingredients which kick-start a sauce are great. A good-quality passata sauce or canned plum tomatoes can act as the foundation for any sauce, as can a good-quality green or red pesto. Other handy store cupboard additions include tapenade, mustard and anchovies. These ingredients have very distinctive tastes and are particularly flavoursome. Roasted red pepper sauce and sundried tomato purée, which tends to be sweeter and more intensely flavoured than regular tomato purée, are also very useful.

Vinegar is another worthwhile store cupboard essential and with so many uses it is worth splashing out on really good quality balsamic and wine vinegars. Herbs and spices are also a must. Using herbs when cooking at home should reduce the temptation to buy ready-made sauces. Often these types of sauces contain large amounts of sugar and additives.

Yeast extract is also a good store cupboard ingredient, which can pep up sauces, soups and casseroles and adds a little substance, particularly to vegetarian dishes.

Eastern flavours offer a lot of scope where low-fat cooking is concerned. Flavourings such as fish sauce, soy sauce, red and green curry paste and Chinese rice wine all offer mouthwatering low-fat flavours to any dish.

For those who are incredibly short on time, or who rarely shop, it is now possible to purchase a selection of readily prepared freshly minced garlic, ginger and chilli. These are available in jars which can be kept in the refrigerator.

As well as these store cupboard additions, many shops and especially supermarkets provide a wide choice of foods. Where possible, invest in the leanest cut of meat and substitute saturated fats such as cream, butter and cheese with low-fat or half-fat alternatives.

Hygiene in the Kitchen

It is important to remember that many foods can carry some form of bacteria. In most cases, the worst it will lead to is a bout of food poisoning or gastroenteritis, although for certain people this can be serious. The risk can be reduced or eliminated, however, by good hygiene and proper cooking.

Do not buy food that is past its sell-by date and do not consume food that is past its use-by date. When buying food, use the eyes and nose. If the food looks tired, limp or a bad colour or it has a rank, acrid or simply bad smell, do not buy or eat it under any circumstances.

Take special care when preparing raw meat and fish. A separate chopping board should be used for each, and the knife, board and your hands should be thoroughly washed before handling or preparing any other food.

Regularly clean, defrost and clear out the refrigerator or freezer – it is worth checking the packaging to see exactly how long each product is safe to freeze. Avoid handling food if suffering from an upset stomach as bacteria can be

passed on through food preparation.

Dish cloths and tea towels must be washed and changed regularly. Ideally use disposable cloths which should be replaced on a daily basis. More durable cloths should be left to soak in bleach, then washed in the washing machine at a high temperature.

Keep your hands, cooking utensils and food preparation surfaces clean and do not allow pets to climb on to any work surfaces.

Buying

Avoid bulk buying where possible, especially fresh produce such as meat, poultry, fish, fruit and vegetables. Fresh foods lose their nutritional value rapidly, so buying a little at a time minimises loss of nutrients. It also means your fridge won't be so full, which reduces the effectiveness of the refrigeration process.

When buying prepackaged goods such as cans or pots of cream and yogurts, check that the packaging is intact and not damaged or pierced at all. Cans should not be dented, pierced or rusty. Check the sell-by dates even for cans and packets of dry ingredients such as flour and rice. Store fresh foods in the refrigerator as soon as possible – not in the car or the office.

When buying frozen foods, ensure that they are not heavily iced on the outside and that the contents feel completely frozen. Ensure that the frozen foods have been stored in the cabinet at the correct storage level and the temperature is below -18°C/ -0.4°F. Pack in cool bags to transport home and place in the freezer as soon as possible after purchase.

Preparation

Make sure that all work surfaces and utensils are clean and dry. Hygiene should be given priority at all times. Separate chopping boards should be used for raw and cooked

meats, fish and vegetables. Currently, a variety of good quality plastic boards come in various designs and colours. This makes differentiating easier and the plastic has the added hygienic advantage of being washable at high temperatures in the dishwasher. If using the board for fish, first wash in cold water, then in hot to prevent odour. Also remember that knives and utensils should always be thoroughly cleaned after use.

When cooking, be particularly careful to keep cooked and raw food separate to avoid any contamination. It is worth washing all fruits and vegetables regardless of whether they are going to be eaten raw or lightly cooked. This rule should apply even to prewashed herbs and salads.

Do not reheat food more than once. If using a microwave, always check that the food is piping hot all the way through – in theory, the food should reach 70°C/158°F and needs to be cooked at that temperature for at least three minutes to ensure that all bacteria are killed.

All poultry must be thoroughly thawed before using, including chicken and poussin. Remove the food to be thawed from the freezer and place in a shallow dish to contain the juices. Leave the food in the refrigerator until it is completely thawed. A 1.4 kg/3 lb whole chicken will take about 26–30 hours to thaw. To speed up the process, immerse the chicken in cold water, making sure that the water is changed regularly. When the joints can move freely and no ice crystals remain in the cavity, the bird is completely thawed.

Once thawed, remove the wrapper and pat the chicken dry. Place the chicken in a shallow dish, cover lightly and store as close to the base of the refrigerator as possible. The chicken should be cooked as soon as possible. Some foods can be cooked from frozen including many prepacked foods such as soups, sauces, casseroles and breads. Where applicable follow the manufacturers' instructions.

Vegetables and fruits can also be cooked from frozen, but meats and fish should be thawed first. The only time food can be refrozen is when the food has been thoroughly thawed then cooked. Once the food has cooled then it can be frozen again, but it should only be stored for one month.

All poultry and game (except for duck) must be cooked thoroughly. When cooked, the juices will run clear on the thickest part of the bird – the best area to try is usually the thigh. Other meats, like minced meat and pork should be cooked right the way through. Fish should turn opaque, be firm in texture and break easily into large flakes.

When cooking leftovers, make sure they are reheated until piping hot and that any sauce or soup reaches boiling point first.

Storing, Refrigerating and Freezing

Meat, poultry, fish, seafood and dairy products should all be refrigerated. The temperature of the refrigerator should be between 1–5°C/34–41°F while the freezer temperature should not rise above -18°C/-0.4°F.

To ensure the optimum refrigerator and freezer temperature, avoid leaving the door open for long periods of time. Try not to overstock the refrigerator as this reduces the airflow inside and therefore the effectiveness in cooling the food within.

When refrigerating cooked food, allow it to cool down quickly and completely before refrigerating. Hot food will raise the temperature of the refrigerator and possibly affect or spoil other food stored in it.

Food within the refrigerator and freezer should always be covered. Raw and cooked food should be stored in separate parts of the refrigerator. Cooked food should be kept on the top shelves of the refrigerator, while raw meat, poultry and fish should be placed on bottom shelves to avoid

drips and cross-contamination. It is recommended that eggs should be refrigerated in order to maintain their freshness and shelf life.

Take care that frozen foods are not stored in the freezer for too long. Blanched vegetables can be stored for one month; beef, lamb, poultry and pork for six months and unblanched vegetables and fruits in syrup for a year. Oily fish and sausages should be stored for three months. Dairy products can last four to six months, while cakes and pastries should be kept in the freezer for three to six months.

High Risk Foods

Certain foods may carry risks to people who are considered vulnerable such as the elderly, the ill, pregnant women, babies, young infants and those suffering from a recurring illness.

It is advisable to avoid those foods listed below which belong to a higher-risk category.

There is a slight chance that some eggs carry the bacteria salmonella. Cook the eggs until both the yolk and the white are firm to eliminate this risk. Pay particular attention to dishes and products incorporating lightly cooked or raw eggs which should be eliminated from the diet. Hollandaise sauce, mayonnaise, mousses, soufflés and meringues all use raw or lightly cooked eggs, as do custard-based dishes, ice creams and sorbets. These are all considered high-risk foods to the vulnerable groups mentioned above.

Certain meats and poultry also carry the potential risk of salmonella and so should be cooked thoroughly

until the juices run clear and there is no pinkness left. Unpasteurised products such as milk, cheese (especially soft cheese), pâté, meat (both raw and cooked) all have the potential risk of listeria and should be avoided.

When buying seafood, buy from a reputable source which has a high turnover to ensure freshness. Fish should have bright clear eyes, shiny skin and bright pink or red gills. The fish should feel stiff to the touch, with a slight smell of sea air and iodine. The flesh of fish steaks and fillets should be translucent with no signs of discolouration. Molluscs such as scallops, clams and mussels are sold fresh and are still alive. Avoid any that are open or do not close when tapped lightly. In the same way, univalves such as cockles or winkles should withdraw back into their shells when lightly prodded. When choosing cephalopods such as squid and octopus they should have a firm flesh and pleasant sea smell.

As with all fish, whether it is shellfish or seafish, care is required when freezing it. It is imperative to check whether the fish has been frozen before. If it has been frozen, then it should not be frozen again under any circumstances.

Guidelines for Different Age Groups

Good food plays such an important role in everyone's life. From infancy through to adulthood, a healthy diet provides the body's foundation and building blocks and teaches children healthy eating habits. Studies have shown that these eating habits stay with us into later life helping us to maintain a healthier lifestyle as adults. This reduces the risk of illness, disease and certain medical problems.

Striking a healthy balance is important and at certain stages in life, this balance may need to be adjusted to help our bodies cope. As babies and children, during pregnancy and in later life, our diet assists us in achieving optimal health. So how do we go about achieving this?

We know that foods such as oily fish, for example, are advantageous to everyone, as they are rich in Omega-3 fatty acids which have been linked with more efficient brain functioning and better memory. They can also help lower the risk of cancer and heart disease. But are there any other steps we can take to maximise health benefits through our diet?

Babies and Young Children

Babies should not be given solids until they are at least six months old, then new tastes and textures can be introduced to their diets. Probably the easiest and cheapest way is to adapt the food that the rest of the family eat. Babies under the age of one should be given breast milk or formula milk. From the age of one to two, whole milk should be given and from two to five semi-skimmed milk can be given. From then on, skimmed milk can be introduced if desired.

The first foods for babies under six months should be of a purée-like consistency, which is smooth and fairly liquid, therefore making it easy to swallow. This can be done using an electric blender, a hand blender or just by pushing foods through a sieve to remove any lumps. Remember, however, babies still need high levels of milk.

Babies over six months old should still be having puréed food, but the consistency of their diet can be made progressively lumpier. Around the 10-month mark, most babies are able to manage food cut up into small pieces.

So, what food groups do babies and small children need? Like adults, a high proportion of their diet should contain grains such as cereal, pasta, bread and rice. Be careful, however, as babies and small children cannot cope with too much high-fibre food in their diet.

Fresh fruits and vegetables should be introduced, as well as a balance of dairy and meat proteins and only a small proportion of fats and sweets. Research points out that delaying the introduction of foods which could cause allergies during the first year (such as cow's milk, wheat, eggs, cheese, yogurt and nuts) can significantly reduce the risk of certain food allergies later on in life. Peanuts should never be given to children under five years old.

Seek a doctor or health visitor's advice regarding babies and toddlers. Limit sugar in young children's diets, as sugar provides only empty calories. Use less processed sugars (muscovado is very sweet, so the amount used can be reduced) or incorporate less-refined alternatives such as dried fruits, dates, rice syrup or honey, although honey should not be given to infants under one year of age.

As in a low-fat diet, it is best to eliminate fried foods and avoid adding salt – especially for under one-year-olds and young infants. Instead, introduce herbs and gentle spices to make food appetising. The more varied the tastes that children experience in their formative years, the wider the range of foods they will accept later in life.

Pregnancy

During pregnancy, women are advised to take extra vitamin and mineral supplements. Pregnant women benefit from a healthy balanced diet, rich in fresh fruit and vegetables, and full of essential vitamins and minerals. Occasionally eating oily fish, such as salmon, not only gives the body essential fats but also provides high levels of bio-available calcium.

Certain food groups, however, hold risks during pregnancy. This section gives advice on everyday foods and those that should be avoided.

Cheese

Pregnant women should avoid all soft, mould-ripened cheese such as Brie. Also if pregnant, do not eat cheese such as Parmesan or blue-veined cheese like Stilton as they carry the risk of listeria. It is fine for pregnant women to carry on eating hard cheese like Cheddar, as well as cottage cheese.

Eggs

There is a slight chance that some eggs will carry salmonella. Cooking the eggs until both the yolk and white are firm will eliminate this risk. However, particular attention should be paid to dishes and products that incorporate lightly cooked or raw eggs – homemade mayonnaise or similar sauces, mousses, soufflés, meringues, ice cream and sorbets. Commercially produced products, such as mayonnaise, which are made with pasteurised eggs, may be eaten safely. If in doubt, play safe and avoid it.

Ready-made Meals and Ready-to-eat Items

Previously cooked, then chilled meals are now widely available, but those from the chilled counter can contain bacteria. Avoid prepacked salads in dressings and other foods which are sold loose from chilled cabinets. Also do not eat raw or partly cooked meats, pâté, unpasteurised milk and soil-dirty fruits and vegetables as they can cause toxoplasmosis.

Meat and Fish

Certain meats and poultry carry the potential risk of salmonella and should be cooked thoroughly until the juices run clear and there is no pinkness left.

Pay particular attention when buying and cooking fish (especially shellfish). Buy only the freshest fish which should smell salty but not strong or fishy.

Look for bright eyes and reject any with sunken eyes. The bodies should look fresh, plump and shiny. Avoid any fish with dry, shrivelled or damp bodies.

It is also best to avoid any shellfish while pregnant unless it is definitely fresh and thoroughly cooked. Shellfish also contains harmful bacteria and viruses.

Later Life

So what about later on in life? As the body gets older, we can help stave off infection and illness through our diet. There is evidence to show that the immune system becomes weaker as we get older, which can increase the risk of suffering from cancer and other illnesses. Maintaining a diet rich in antioxidants, fresh fruits and vegetables, plant oils and oily fish is especially beneficial in order to either prevent these illnesses or minimise their effects. As with all age groups, the body benefits from the five-a-day eating plan – to eat five portions of fruit or vegetables each day. Leafy green vegetables, in particular, are rich in antioxidants. Cabbage, broccoli, Brussels sprouts, cauliflower and kale contain particularly high levels of antioxidants, which lower the risk of cancer.

Foods which are green in colour tend to provide nutrients essential for healthy nerves, muscles and hormones, while foods red in colour protect against cardiovascular disease. Other foods which can also assist in preventing cardiovascular disease and ensuring a healthy heart include vitamins E and C, oily fish and essential fats (such as extra virgin olive oil and garlic). They help lower blood cholesterol levels and clear arteries. A diet high in fresh fruits and vegetables and low in salt and saturated fats can considerably reduce heart disease.

Other foods have recognised properties. Certain types of mushrooms are known to boost the immune system, while garlic not only boosts the immune system but also protects the body against cancer. Live yogurt, too, has healthy properties as it contains gut-friendly bacteria which help digestion.

Some foods can help to balance the body's hormone levels during the menopause. For example, soya regulates hormone levels. Studies have shown that a regular intake of soya can help to protect the body against breast and prostate cancer.

A balanced, healthy diet, rich in fresh fruits and vegetables, carbohydrates, proteins and essential fats and low in saturates, can help the body protect itself throughout your life. It really is worth spending a little extra time and effort when shopping or even just thinking about what to cook.

Hot Tiger Prawns with Parma Ham

INGREDIENTS

Serves 4

½ cucumber, peeled if preferred
4 ripe tomatoes
12 raw tiger prawns
6 tbsp olive oil
4 garlic cloves, peeled and crushed
4 tbsp freshly chopped parsley
salt and freshly ground black pepper
6 slices of Parma ham, cut in half
4 slices flat Italian bread
4 tbsp dry white wine

HELPFUL HINT

The black intestinal vein needs to be removed from raw prawns because it can cause a bitter flavour. Remove the shell, then using a small, sharp knife, make a cut along the centre back of the prawn and open out the flesh. Using the tip of the knife, remove the thread that lies along the length of the prawn and discard.

1. Preheat oven to 180°C/350°F/Gas Mark 4. Slice the cucumber and tomatoes thinly, then arrange on four large plates and reserve. Peel the prawns, leaving the tail shell intact and remove the thin black vein running down the back.

2. Whisk together 4 tablespoons of the olive oil, garlic and chopped parsley in a small bowl and season to taste with plenty of salt and pepper. Add the prawns to the mixture and stir until they are well coated. Remove the prawns, then wrap each one in a piece of Parma ham and secure with a cocktail stick.

3. Place the prepared prawns on a lightly oiled baking sheet or dish with the slices of bread and cook in the preheated oven for 5 minutes.

4. Remove the prawns from the oven and spoon the wine over the prawns and bread. Return to the oven and cook for a further 10 minutes until piping hot.

5. Carefully remove the cocktail sticks and arrange three prawn rolls on each slice of bread. Place on top of the sliced cucumber and tomatoes and serve immediately.

2

3

4

Potato Pancakes with Smoked Salmon

INGREDIENTS

Serves 4

450 g/1 lb floury potatoes, peeled
  and quartered
salt and freshly ground black pepper
1 large egg
1 large egg yolk
25 g/1 oz butter
25 g/1 oz plain flour
150 ml/¼ pint double cream
2 tbsp freshly chopped parsley
5 tbsp crème fraîche
1 tbsp horseradish sauce
225 g/8 oz smoked salmon, sliced
salad leaves, to serve

To garnish:
lemon slices
snipped chives

TASTY TIP

Horseradish is a pungent root, usually finely grated and mixed with oil and vinegar or cream to make horseradish sauce. Sauces can vary in hotness, so it is best to add a little at a time to the crème fraîche and taste until you have the desired flavour.

1   Cook the potatoes in a saucepan of lightly salted boiling water for 15–20 minutes, or until tender. Drain thoroughly, then mash until free of lumps. Beat in the whole egg and egg yolk, together with the butter. Beat until smooth and creamy. Slowly beat in the flour and cream, then season to taste with salt and pepper. Stir in the chopped parsley.

2   Beat the crème fraîche and horseradish sauce together in a small bowl, cover with clingfilm and reserve.

3   Heat a lightly oiled, heavy-based frying pan over a medium-high heat. Place a few spoonfuls of the potato mixture in the hot pan and cook for 4–5 minutes, or until cooked and golden, turning halfway through cooking time. Remove from the pan, drain on absorbent kitchen paper and keep warm. Repeat with the remaining mixture.

4   Arrange the pancakes on individual serving plates. Place the smoked salmon on the pancakes and spoon over a little of the horseradish sauce. Serve with salad and the remaining horseradish sauce and garnish with lemon slices and chives.

1

2

3

Crispy Prawns with Chinese Dipping Sauce

INGREDIENTS

Serves 4

450 g/1 lb medium-sized raw
  prawns, peeled

¼ tsp salt

6 tbsp groundnut oil

2 garlic cloves, peeled and
  finely chopped

2.5 cm/1 inch piece fresh root ginger,
  peeled and finely chopped

1 green chilli, deseeded and
  finely chopped

4 stems fresh coriander, leaves and
  stems roughly chopped

For the chinese dipping sauce:

3 tbsp dark soy sauce

3 tbsp rice wine vinegar

1 tbsp caster sugar

2 tbsp chilli oil

2 spring onions, finely shredded

1. Using a sharp knife, remove the black vein along the back of the prawns. Sprinkle the prawns with the salt and leave to stand for 15 minutes. Pat dry on absorbent kitchen paper.

2. Heat a wok or large frying pan, add the groundnut oil and when hot, add the prawns and stir-fry in 2 batches for about 1 minute, or until they turn pink and are almost cooked. Using a slotted spoon, remove the prawns and keep warm in a low oven.

3. Drain the oil from the wok, leaving 1 tablespoon. Add the garlic, ginger and chilli and cook for about 30 seconds. Add the coriander, return the prawns and stir-fry for 1–2 minutes, or until the prawns are cooked through and the garlic is golden. Turn into a warmed serving dish.

4. For the dipping sauce, using a fork, beat together the soy sauce, rice vinegar, caster sugar and chilli oil in a small bowl. Stir in the spring onions. Serve immediately with the hot prawns.

2

3

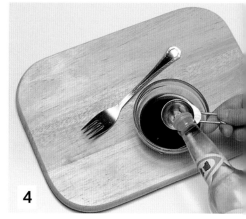

4

Sesame Prawn Toasts

INGREDIENTS

Serves 4

125 g/4 oz peeled cooked prawns
1 tbsp cornflour
2 spring onions, peeled and
   roughly chopped
2 tsp freshly grated root ginger
2 tsp dark soy sauce
pinch of Chinese five spice
   powder (optional)
1 small egg, beaten
salt and freshly ground black pepper
6 thin slices day-old white bread
40 g/1½ oz sesame seeds
vegetable oil for deep-frying
chilli sauce, to serve

HELPFUL HINT

The toasts can be prepared to the end of step 3 up to 12 hours in advance. Cover and chill in the refrigerator until needed. It is important to use bread that is a day or two old and not fresh bread. Make sure that the prawns are well-drained before puréeing – pat them dry on absorbent kitchen paper, if necessary.

1   Place the prawns in a food processor or blender with the cornflour, spring onions, ginger, soy sauce and Chinese five spice powder, if using. Blend to a fairly smooth paste. Spoon into a bowl and stir in the beaten egg. Season to taste with salt and pepper.

2   Cut the crusts off the bread. Spread the prawn paste in an even layer on one side of each slice. Sprinkle over the sesame seeds and press down lightly.

3   Cut each slice diagonally into four triangles. Place on a board and chill in the refrigerator for 30 minutes.

4   Pour sufficient oil into a heavy-based saucepan or deep-fat fryer so that it is one-third full. Heat until it reaches a temperature of 180°C/350°F. Cook the toasts in batches of five or six, carefully lowering them seeded-side down into the oil. Deep-fry for 2–3 minutes, or until lightly browned, then turn over and cook for 1 minute more. Using a slotted spoon, lift out the toasts and drain on absorbent kitchen paper. Keep warm while frying the remaining toasts. Arrange on a warmed platter and serve immediately with some chilli sauce for dipping.

1

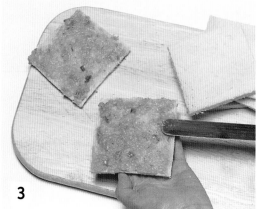

3

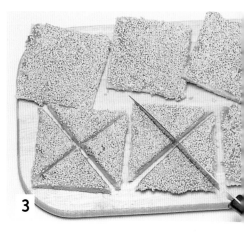

3

Fish Puff Tart

INGREDIENTS

Serves 4

350 g/12 oz prepared puff pastry,
  thawed if frozen
150 g/5 oz smoked haddock
150 g/5 oz cod
1 tbsp pesto sauce
2 tomatoes, sliced
125 g/4 oz goats' cheese, sliced
1 medium egg, beaten
freshly chopped parsley, to garnish

FOOD FACT

The Scottish name for smoked haddock is finnan haddie, named after the Scottish fishing village of Findon near Aberdeen. Smoked haddock has been a favourite breakfast dish in Findon and the rest of Scotland for many years. Although this type of fish was traditionally caught and smoked (sometimes over peat fires) in Scotland, nowadays the fish is produced in New England and other eastern coastal states of the United States.

1 Preheat the oven to 220°C/425°F/Gas Mark 7. On a lightly floured surface roll out the pastry into a 20.5 x 25.5 cm/8 x 10 inch rectangle.

2 Draw a 18 x 23 cm/7 x 9 inch rectangle in the centre of the pastry, to form a 2.5 cm/1 inch border. Be careful not to cut through the pastry.

3 Lightly cut criss-cross patterns in the border of the pastry with a knife.

4 Place the fish on a chopping board and with a sharp knife skin the cod and smoked haddock. Cut into thin slices.

5 Spread the pesto evenly over the bottom of the pastry case with the back of a spoon.

6 Arrange the fish, tomatoes and cheese in the pastry case and brush the pastry with the beaten egg.

7 Bake the tart in the preheated oven for 20–25 minutes, until the pastry is well risen, puffed and golden brown. Garnish with the chopped parsley and serve immediately.

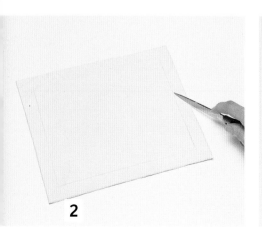

2

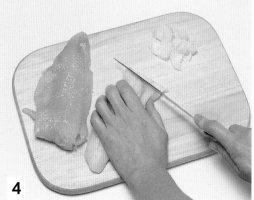

4

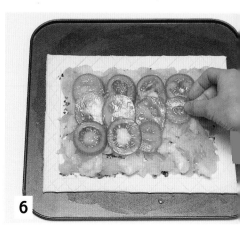

6

Smoked Mackerel Vol–au–Vents

INGREDIENTS

Serves 4

350 g/12 oz prepared puff pastry
1 small egg, beaten
2 tsp sesame seeds
225 g/8 oz peppered smoked
   mackerel, skinned and chopped
5 cm/2 inch piece cucumber
4 tbsp soft cream cheese
2 tbsp cranberry sauce
1 tbsp freshly chopped dill
1 tbsp finely grated lemon rind
dill sprigs, to garnish
mixed salad leaves, to serve

FOOD FACT

Mackerel is a relatively cheap fish and one of the richest sources of minerals, oils and vitamins available. This dish is an affordable way to incorporate all these essential nutrients into your diet.

1 Preheat the oven to 230°C/450°F/Gas Mark 8. Roll the pastry out on a lightly floured surface and using a 9 cm/3½ inch fluted cutter cut out 12 rounds.

2 Using a 1 cm/½ inch cutter, mark a lid in the centre of each round.

3 Place on a damp baking sheet and brush the rounds with a little beaten egg.

4 Sprinkle the pastry with the sesame seeds and bake in the preheated oven for 10–12 minutes, or until golden brown and well risen.

5 Transfer the vol-au-vents to a chopping board and when cool enough to touch carefully remove the lids with a small sharp knife.

6 Scoop out any uncooked pastry from the inside of each vol-au-vent, then return to the oven for 5–8 minutes to dry out. Remove and allow to cool.

7 Flake the mackerel into small pieces and reserve. Peel the cucumber if desired, cut into very small dice and add to the mackerel.

8 Beat the soft cream cheese with the cranberry sauce, dill and lemon rind. Stir in the mackerel and cucumber and use to fill the vol-au-vents. Place the lids on top and garnish dill sprigs.

1

5

8

Smoked Haddock Tart

INGREDIENTS

Serves 6

Shortcrust pastry:

150 g/5 oz plain flour

pinch of salt

25 g/1 oz lard or white vegetable fat,
   cut into small cubes

40 g/1½ oz butter or hard margarine,
   cut into small cubes

For the filling:

225 g/8 oz smoked haddock, skinned
   and cubed

2 large eggs, beaten

300 ml/½ pint double cream

1 tsp Dijon mustard

freshly ground black pepper

125 g/4 oz Gruyère cheese, grated

1 tbsp freshly snipped chives

To serve:

lemon wedges

tomato wedges

fresh green salad leaves

1 Preheat the oven to 190°C/375°F/Gas Mark 5. Sift the flour and salt into a large bowl. Add the fats and mix lightly. Using the fingertips rub into the flour until the mixture resembles breadcrumbs.

2 Sprinkle 1 tablespoon of cold water into the mixture and with a knife, start bringing the dough together. It may be necessary to use your hands for the final stage. If the dough does not form a ball instantly, add a little more water.

3 Put the pastry in a polythene bag and chill for at least 30 minutes.

4 On a lightly floured surface, roll out the pastry and use to line a 18 cm/7 inch lightly oiled quiche or flan tin. Prick the base all over with a fork and bake blind in the preheated oven for 15 minutes.

5 Carefully remove the pastry from the oven and brush with a little of the beaten egg.

6 Return to the oven for a further 5 minutes, then place the fish in the pastry case.

7 For the filling, beat together the eggs and cream. Add the mustard, black pepper and cheese and pour over the fish.

8 Sprinkle with the chives and bake for 35–40 minutes or until the filling is golden brown and set in the centre. Serve hot or cold with the lemon and tomato wedges and salad leaves.

2

5

7

Marinated Mackerel with Tomato & Basil Salad

INGREDIENTS

Serves 3

3 mackerel, filleted
3 beefsteak tomatoes, sliced
50 g/2 oz watercress
2 oranges, peeled and segmented
75 g/3 oz mozzarella cheese, sliced
2 tbsp basil leaves, shredded
sprig of fresh basil, to garnish

For the marinade:
juice of 2 lemons
4 tbsp olive oil
4 tbsp basil leaves

For the dressing:
1 tbsp lemon juice
1 tsp Dijon mustard
1 tsp caster sugar
salt and freshly ground black pepper
5 tbsp olive oil

1 Remove as many of the fine pin bones as possible from the mackerel fillets, lightly rinse and pat dry with absorbent kitchen paper and place in a shallow dish.

2 Blend the marinade ingredients together and pour over the mackerel fillets. Make sure the marinade has covered the fish completely. Cover and leave in a cool place for at least 8 hours, but preferably overnight. As the fillets marinate, they will loose the translucency and look as if they are cooked.

3 Place the tomatoes, watercress, oranges and mozzarella cheese in a large bowl and toss.

4 To make the dressing, whisk the lemon juice with the mustard, sugar and seasoning in a bowl. Pour over half the dressing, toss again and then arrange on a serving platter. Remove the mackerel from the marinade, cut into bite-sized pieces and sprinkle with the shredded basil. Arrange on top of the salad, drizzle over the remaining dressing, scatter with basil leaves and garnish with a basil sprig. Serve.

1

2

4

Luxury Fish Pasties

INGREDIENTS

Serves 6

450 g/1 lb shop-bought flaky pastry
125 g/4 oz butter
125 g/4oz plain flour
300 ml/½ pint milk
225 g/8 oz salmon fillet, skinned
  and cut into chunks
1 tbsp freshly chopped parsley
1 tbsp freshly chopped dill
grated rind and juice of 1 lime
225 g/8 oz peeled prawns
salt and freshly ground black pepper
1 small egg, beaten
1 tsp sea salt
fresh green salad leaves, to serve

HELPFUL HINT

Salmon is not only full of minerals but is a vital source of calcium as well as being extremely low in fat. Ensure when using raw prawns that the vein that runs along the back of the prawn is removed.

1 Preheat the oven to 200°C/400°F/Gas Mark 6. Place the butter in a saucepan and slowly heat until melted.

2 Add the flour and cook, stirring for 1 minute. Remove from the heat and gradually add the milk a little at a time, stirring between each addition.

3 Return to the heat and simmer, stirring continuously until thickened. Remove from the heat and add the salmon, parsley, dill, lime rind, lime juice, prawns and seasoning.

4 Roll out the pastry on a lightly floured surface and cut out six 12.5 cm/5 inch circles and six 15 cm/6 inch circles.

5 Brush the edges of the smallest circle with the beaten egg and place 2 tablespoons of filling in the centre of each one.

6 Place the larger circle over the filling and press the edges together to seal.

7 Pinch the edge of the pastry between the forefinger and thumb to ensure a firm seal and decorative edge.

8 Cut a slit in each parcel, brush with the beaten egg and sprinkle with sea salt.

9 Transfer to a baking sheet and cook in the preheated oven for 20 minutes, or until golden brown. Serve immediately with some fresh green salad leaves.

3

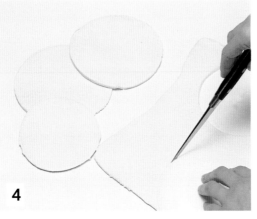

4

7

Sesame Prawns

INGREDIENTS

Serves 6-8

24 large raw prawns
40 g/1 oz plain flour
4 tbsp sesame seeds
salt and freshly ground black pepper
1 large egg
300 ml/½ pint vegetable oil for
    deep frying

For the soy dipping sauce:

50 ml/2 fl oz soy sauce
1 spring onion, trimmed and
    finely chopped
½ tsp dried crushed chillies
1 tbsp sesame oil
1-2 tsp sugar, or to taste
strips of spring onion, to garnish

HELPFUL HINT

Raw prawns are widely available but are cheapest bought frozen in boxes from Asian and Chinese grocers.

1. Remove the heads from the prawns by twisting away from the body and discard. Peel the prawns, leaving the tails on for presentation. Using a sharp knife, remove the black vein from the back of the prawns. Rinse and dry.

2. Slice along the back, but do not cut through the prawn body. Place on the chopping board and press firmly to flatten slightly, to make a butterfly shape.

3. Put the flour, half the sesame seeds, salt and pepper into a food processor and blend for 30 seconds. Tip into a polythene bag and add the prawns, four to five at a time. Twist to seal, then shake to coat with the flour.

4. Beat the egg in a small bowl with the remaining sesame seeds, salt and pepper.

5. Heat the oil in a large wok to 190°C/375°F, or until a small cube of bread browns in about 30 seconds. Working in batches of five or six, and holding each prawn by the tail, dip into the beaten egg, then carefully lower into the oil.

6. Cook for 1–2 minutes, or until crisp and golden, turning once or twice. Using a slotted spoon, remove the prawns, drain on absorbent kitchen paper and keep warm.

7. To make the dipping sauce, stir together the soy sauce, spring onion, chillies, oil and sugar until the sugar dissolves. Arrange the prawns on a plate, garnish with strips of spring onion and serve immediately.

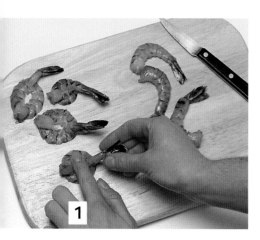

1

3

6

Smoked Salmon Sushi

INGREDIENTS

Serves 4

175 g/6 oz sushi rice
2 tbsp rice vinegar
4 tsp caster sugar
½ tsp salt
2 sheets sushi nori
60 g/2½ oz smoked salmon
¼ cucumber, cut into fine strips

To serve:
wasabi
soy sauce
pickled ginger

TASTY TIP

If wasabi is unavailable, use a little horseradish. If unable to get sushi nori (seaweed sheets), shape the rice into small bite-size oblongs, then drape a piece of smoked salmon over each one and garnish with chives.

1 Rinse the rice thoroughly in cold water, until the water runs clear, then place in a pan with 300 ml/½ pint of water. Bring to the boil and cover with a tight-fitting lid. Reduce to a simmer and cook gently for 10 minutes. Turn the heat off, but keep the pan covered, to allow the rice to steam for a further 10 minutes.

2 In a small saucepan gently heat the rice vinegar, sugar and salt until the sugar has dissolved. When the rice has finished steaming, pour over the vinegar mixture and stir well to mix. Empty the rice out on to a large flat surface – a chopping board or large plate is ideal. Fan the rice to cool and to produce a shinier rice.

3 Lay one sheet of sushi nori on a sushi mat (if you do not have a sushi mat, improvise with a stiff piece of fabric that is a little larger than the sushi nori) and spread with half the cooled rice. Dampen your hands while doing this – it will help to prevent the rice from sticking to them. On the nearest edge place half the salmon and half the cucumber strips.

4 Roll up the rice and smoked salmon into a tight Swiss roll-like shape. Dampen the blade of a sharp knife and cut the sushi into slices about 2 cm/¾ inch thick. Repeat with the remaining sushi nori, rice, smoked salmon and cucumber. Serve with wasabi, soy sauce and pickled ginger.

2

3

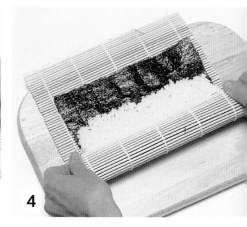

4

Spicy Prawns in Lettuce Cups

INGREDIENTS

Serves 4

1 lemon grass stalk

225 g/8 oz peeled cooked prawns

1 tsp finely grated lime zest

1 red bird's eye chilli, deseeded and
   finely chopped

2.5 cm/1 inch piece fresh root ginger,
   peeled and grated

2 Little Gem lettuces, divided
   into leaves

25 g/1 oz roasted peanuts, chopped

2 spring onions, trimmed and
   diagonally sliced

sprig of fresh coriander, to garnish

For the coconut sauce:

2 tbsp freshly grated or unsweetened
   shredded coconut

1 tbsp hoisin sauce

1 tbsp light soy sauce

1 tbsp Thai fish sauce

1 tbsp palm sugar or
   soft light brown sugar

1 Remove three or four of the tougher outer leaves of the lemon grass and reserve for another dish. Finely chop the remaining softer centre. Place 2 teaspoons of the chopped lemon grass in a bowl with the prawns, grated lime zest, chilli and ginger. Mix together to coat the prawns. Cover and place in the refrigerator to marinate while you make the coconut sauce.

2 For the sauce, place the grated coconut in a wok or nonstick frying pan and dry-fry for 2–3 minutes or until golden. Remove from the pan and reserve. Add the hoisin, soy and fish sauces to the pan with the sugar and 4 tablespoons of water. Simmer for 2–3 minutes, then remove from the heat. Leave to cool.

3 Pour the sauce over the prawns, add the toasted coconut and toss to mix together. Divide the prawn and coconut sauce mixture between the lettuce leaves and arrange on a platter.

4 Sprinkle over the chopped roasted peanuts and spring onions and garnish with a sprig of fresh coriander. Serve immediately.

Crispy Pork Wontons

INGREDIENTS

Serves 4

1 small onion, peeled and
  roughly chopped
2 garlic cloves, peeled and crushed
1 green chilli, deseeded and chopped
2.5 cm/1 inch piece fresh root ginger,
  peeled and roughly chopped
450 g/1 lb lean pork mince
4 tbsp freshly chopped coriander
1 tsp Chinese five spice powder
salt and freshly ground black pepper
20 wonton wrappers
1 medium egg, lightly beaten
vegetable oil for deep-frying
chilli sauce, to serve

1   Place the onion, garlic, chilli and ginger in a food processor and blend until very finely chopped. Add the pork, coriander and Chinese five spice powder. Season to taste with salt and pepper, then blend again briefly to mix. Divide the mixture into 20 equal portions and with floured hands shape each into a walnut-sized ball.

2   Brush the edges of a wonton wrapper with beaten egg, place a pork ball in the centre, then bring the corners to the centre and pinch together to make a money bag. Repeat with the remaining pork balls and wrappers.

3   Pour sufficient oil into a heavy-based saucepan or deep-fat fryer so that it is one-third full and heat to 180°C/350°F. Deep-fry the wontons in three or four batches for 3–4 minutes, or until cooked through and golden and crisp. Drain on absorbent kitchen paper. Serve the crispy pork wontons immediately, allowing five per person, with some chilli sauce for dipping.

1

2

3

Dim Sum Pork Parcels

INGREDIENTS

Makes about 40

125 g/4 oz canned water chestnuts,
  drained and finely chopped

125 g/4 oz raw prawns, peeled,
  deveined and coarsely chopped

350 g/12 oz fresh pork mince

2 tbsp smoked bacon, finely chopped

1 tbsp light soy sauce, plus extra,
  to serve

1 tsp dark soy sauce

1 tbsp Chinese rice wine

2 tbsp fresh root ginger, peeled
  and finely chopped

3 spring onions, trimmed and
  finely chopped

2 tsp sesame oil

1 medium egg white, lightly beaten

salt and freshly ground black pepper

2 tsp sugar

40 wonton skins, thawed if frozen

toasted sesame seeds, to garnish

soy sauce, to serve

1 Place the water chestnuts, prawns, pork mince and bacon in a bowl and mix together. Add the soy sauces, Chinese rice wine, ginger, chopped spring onion, sesame oil and egg white. Season to taste with salt and pepper, sprinkle in the sugar and mix the filling thoroughly.

2 Place a spoonful of filling in the centre of a wonton skin. Bring the sides up and press around the filling to make a basket shape. Flatten the base of the skin, so the wonton stands solid. The top should be wide open, exposing the filling.

3 Place the parcels on a heatproof plate, on a wire rack inside a wok or on the base of a muslin-lined bamboo steamer. Place over a wok, half-filled with boiling water, cover, then steam the parcels for about 20 minutes. Do this in two batches. Transfer to a warmed serving plate, sprinkle with toasted sesame seeds, drizzle with soy sauce and serve immediately.

Bacon, Mushroom & Cheese Puffs

INGREDIENTS

Serves 4

1 tbsp olive oil

225 g/8 oz field mushrooms, wiped
    and roughly chopped

225 g/8 oz rindless streaky bacon,
    roughly chopped

2 tbsp freshly chopped parsley

salt and freshly ground black pepper

350 g/12 oz ready-rolled puff pastry
    sheets, thawed if frozen

25 g/1 oz Emmenthal cheese, grated

1 medium egg, beaten

salad leaves such as rocket or
    watercress, to garnish

tomatoes, to serve

TASTY TIP

The Emmenthal cheese in this recipe can be substituted for any other cheese, but for best results use a cheese such as Cheddar, which like Emmenthal melts easily. The bacon can also be substituted for slices of sweeter cured hams such as pancetta, speck, Parma or prosciutto.

1   Preheat the oven to 200°C/400°F/Gas Mark 6. Heat the olive oil in a large frying pan.

2   Add the mushrooms and bacon and fry for 6–8 minutes until golden in colour. Stir in the parsley, season to taste with salt and pepper and allow to cool.

3   Roll the sheet of pastry a little thinner on a lightly floured surface to a 30.5 cm/12 inch square. Cut the pastry into four equal squares.

4   Stir the grated Emmenthal cheese into the mushroom mixture. Spoon a quarter of the mixture on to one half of each square.

5   Brush the edges of the square with a little of the beaten egg.

6   Fold over the pastry to form a triangular parcel. Seal the edges well and place on a lightly oiled baking sheet. Repeat until the squares are done

7   Make shallow slashes in the top of the pastry with a knife.

8   Brush the parcels with the remaining beaten egg and cook in the preheated oven for 20 minutes, or until puffy and golden brown.

9   Serve warm or cold, garnished with the salad leaves and served with tomatoes.

2

4

7

Crostini with Chicken Livers

INGREDIENTS

Serves 4

2 tbsp olive oil

2 tbsp butter

1 shallot, peeled and finely chopped

1 garlic clove, peeled and crushed

150 g/5 oz chicken livers

1 tbsp plain flour

2 tbsp dry white wine

1 tbsp brandy

50 g/2 oz mushrooms, sliced

salt and freshly ground black pepper

4 slices of ciabatta or similar bread

To garnish:

fresh sage leaves

lemon wedges

TASTY TIP

If you prefer a lower fat alternative to the fried bread in this recipe, omit 1 tablespoon of the butter and brush the bread slices with the remaining 1 tablespoon of oil. Bake in a preheated oven 180°C/350°F/Gas Mark 4 for about 20 minutes, or until golden and crisp then serve as above.

1. Heat 1 tablespoon of the olive oil and 1 tablespoon of the butter in a frying pan, add the shallot and garlic and cook gently for 2–3 minutes.

2. Trim and wash the chicken livers thoroughly and pat dry on absorbent kitchen paper as much as possible. Cut into slices, then toss in the flour. Add the livers to the frying pan with the shallot and garlic and continue to fry for a further 2 minutes, stirring continuously.

3. Pour in the white wine and brandy and bring to the boil. Boil rapidly for 1–2 minutes to allow the alcohol to evaporate, then stir in the sliced mushrooms and cook gently for about 5 minutes, or until the chicken livers are cooked, but just a little pink inside. Season to taste with salt and pepper.

4. Fry the slices of ciabatta or similar-style bread in the remaining oil and butter, then place on individual serving dishes. Spoon over the liver mixture and garnish with a few sage leaves and lemon wedges. Serve immediately.

2

3

3

Deep-fried Chicken Wings

INGREDIENTS

Serves 4

2 tsp turmeric

1 tsp hot chilli powder

1 tsp ground coriander

1 tsp ground cumin

3 garlic cloves, peeled and crushed

8 chicken wings

2 tbsp orange marmalade

2 tbsp ginger preserve or marmalade

1 tsp salt

3 tbsp rice wine vinegar

2 tbsp tomato ketchup

1 litre/1¾ pints vegetable oil for
   deep frying

lime wedges, to garnish

HELPFUL HINT

It is important to test the oil to make sure it is at the right temperature. If the oil is not hot enough, the chicken will be greasy but if it is too hot, the food may burn without being properly cooked through.

1 Blend the turmeric, chilli powder, ground coriander, ground cumin and garlic together in a small bowl. Dry the chicken wings thoroughly, using absorbent kitchen paper, then rub the spice mixture onto the skin of each chicken wing. Cover and chill in the refrigerator for at least 2 hours.

2 Meanwhile make the dipping sauce, by mixing together the marmalade, ginger preserve, salt, rice wine vinegar and tomato ketchup in a small saucepan. Heat until blended, leave to cool, then serve. If using straight away, spoon into a small dipping bowl, but if using later pour into a container with a close-fitting lid and store in the refrigerator.

3 Pour the oil into the wok and heat to 190°C/375°F, or until a small cube of bread dropped in the oil turns golden brown in 30 seconds. Cook two to three chicken wings at a time, lowering them into the hot oil, and frying for 3–4 minutes. Remove the wings, using a slotted spoon, and drain on absorbent kitchen paper. You may need to reheat the oil before cooking each batch.

4 When all the chicken wings are cooked, arrange on a warmed serving dish, garnish with the lime wedges and serve.

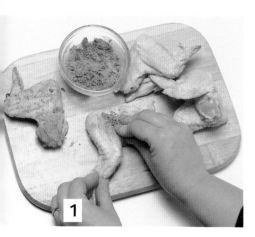

1

2

3

Chicken & Lamb Satay

INGREDIENTS

Makes 16

225 g/8 oz skinless, boneless chicken
225 g/8 oz lean lamb

For the marinade:
1 small onion, peeled and
   finely chopped
2 garlic cloves, peeled and crushed
2.5 cm/1 inch piece fresh root ginger,
   peeled and grated
4 tbsp soy sauce
1 tsp ground coriander
2 tsp dark brown sugar
2 tbsp lime juice
1 tbsp vegetable oil

For the peanut sauce:
300 ml/½ pint coconut milk
4 tbsp crunchy peanut butter
1 tbsp Thai fish sauce
1 tsp lime juice
1 tbsp chilli powder
1 tbsp brown sugar
salt and freshly ground black pepper

To garnish:
sprigs of fresh coriander
lime wedges

1 Preheat the grill just before cooking. Soak the bamboo skewers for 30 minutes before required. Cut the chicken and lamb into thin strips, about 7.5 cm/3 inches long and place in two shallow dishes. Blend all the marinade ingredients together, then pour half over the chicken and half over the lamb. Stir until lightly coated, then cover with clingfilm and leave to marinate in the refrigerator for at least 2 hours, turning occasionally.

2 Remove the chicken and lamb from the marinade and thread on to the skewers. Reserve the marinade. Cook under the preheated grill for 8–10 minutes or until cooked, turning and brushing with the marinade.

3 Meanwhile, make the peanut sauce. Blend the coconut milk with the peanut butter, fish sauce, lime juice, chilli powder and sugar. Pour into a saucepan and cook gently for 5 minutes, stirring occasionally, then season to taste with salt and pepper. Garnish with coriander sprigs and lime wedges and serve the satays with the prepared sauce.

1

2

3

Wild Garlic Mushrooms with Pizza Breadsticks

INGREDIENTS

Serves 6

For the breadsticks:

7 g/¼ oz dried yeast
250 ml/8 fl oz warm water
400 g/14 oz strong, plain flour
2 tbsp olive oil
1 tsp salt

9 tbsp olive oil
4 garlic cloves, peeled and crushed
450 g/1 lb mixed wild mushrooms,
   wiped and dried
salt and freshly ground black pepper
1 tbsp freshly chopped parsley
1 tbsp freshly chopped basil
1 tsp fresh oregano leaves
juice of 1 lemon

HELPFUL HINT

Never clean mushrooms under running water. Mushrooms absorb liquid very easily and then release it again during cooking, making the dish watery. When using wild mushrooms, wipe with a damp cloth or use a soft brush.

1. Preheat oven to 240°C/475°F/Gas Mark 9, 15 minutes before baking. Place the dried yeast in the warm water for 10 minutes. Place the flour in a large bowl and gradually blend in the olive oil, salt and the dissolved yeast.

2. Knead on a lightly floured surface to form a smooth and pliable dough. Cover with clingfilm and leave in a warm place for 15 minutes to allow the dough to rise, then roll out again and cut into sticks of equal length. Cover and leave to rise again for 10 minutes. Brush with the olive oil, sprinkle with salt and bake in the preheated oven for 10 minutes.

3. Pour 3 tablespoons of the oil into a frying pan and add the crushed garlic. Cook over a very low heat, stirring well for 3–4 minutes to flavour the oil.

4. Cut the wild mushrooms into bite-sized slices if very large, then add to the pan. Season well with salt and pepper and cook very gently for 6–8 minutes, or until tender.

5. Whisk the fresh herbs, the remaining olive oil and lemon juice together. Pour over the mushrooms and heat through. Season to taste and place on individual serving dishes. Serve with the pizza breadsticks.

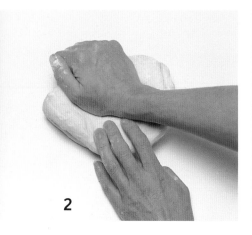

2

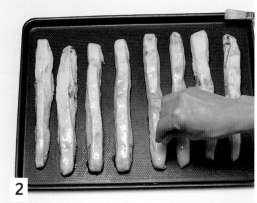

2

4

Bruschetta with Pecorino, Garlic & Tomatoes

INGREDIENTS

Serves 4

6 ripe but firm tomatoes

125 g/4 oz pecorino cheese, finely grated

1 tbsp oregano leaves

salt and freshly ground black pepper

3 tbsp olive oil

3 garlic cloves, peeled

8 slices of flat Italian bread, such as focaccia

50 g/2 oz mozzarella cheese

marinated black olives, to serve

TASTY TIP

Bitter leaves are excellent with these bruschettas because they help to offset the richness of the cheese and tomato topping. Try a mixture of frisée, radicchio and rocket. If these are unavailable, use a bag of mixed salad leaves.

1 Preheat the grill and line the grill rack with tinfoil just before cooking. Make a small cross in the top of the tomatoes, then place in a small bowl and cover with boiling water. Leave to stand for 2 minutes, then drain and remove the skins. Cut into quarters, remove the seeds, and chop the flesh into small dice.

2 Mix the tomato flesh with the pecorino cheese and 2 teaspoons of the fresh oregano and season to taste with salt and pepper. Add 1 tablespoon of the olive oil and mix thoroughly.

3 Crush the garlic and spread evenly over the slices of bread. Heat 2 tablespoons of the olive oil in a large frying pan and sauté the bread slices until they are crisp and golden.

4 Place the fried bread on a lightly oiled baking tray and spoon on the tomato and cheese topping. Place a little mozzarella on top and place under the preheated grill for 3–4 minutes, until golden and bubbling. Garnish with the remaining oregano, then arrange the bruschettas on a serving plate and serve immediately with the olives.

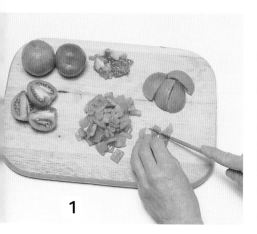

1

2

3

Mozzarella Parcels with Cranberry Relish

INGREDIENTS

Serves 6

125 g/4 oz mozzarella cheese
8 slices of thin white bread
2 medium eggs, beaten
salt and freshly ground black pepper
300 ml/½ pint olive oil

For the relish:

125 g/4 oz cranberries
2 tbsp fresh orange juice
grated rind of 1 small orange
50 g/2 oz soft light brown sugar
1 tbsp port

HELPFUL HINT

Frying in oil that is not hot enough causes food to absorb more oil than it would if fried at the correct temperature. To test the temperature without a thermometer, drop a cube of bread into the frying pan. If the bread browns in 30 seconds the oil is at the right temperature. If it does not, try again in a couple of minutes or increase the heat. If the bread goes very dark, decrease the heat and add about 150 ml/¼ pint of cold oil and test again.

1 Slice the mozzarella thinly, remove the crusts from the bread and make sandwiches with the bread and cheese. Cut into 5 cm/2 inch squares and squash them quite flat. Season the eggs with salt and pepper, then soak the bread in the seasoned egg for 1 minute on each side until well coated.

2 Heat the oil to 190°C/375°F and deep-fry the bread squares for 1–2 minutes, or until they are crisp and golden brown. Drain on absorbent kitchen paper and keep warm while the cranberry relish is prepared.

3 Place the cranberries, orange juice, rind, sugar and port into a small saucepan and add 5 tablespoons of water. Bring to the boil, then simmer for 10 minutes, or until the cranberries have 'popped'. Sweeten with a little more sugar if necessary.

4 Arrange the mozzarella parcels on individual serving plates. Serve with a little of the cranberry relish.

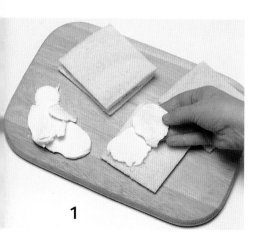

1

1

3

Vegetable Thai Spring Rolls

INGREDIENTS

Serves 4

50 g/2 oz cellophane vermicelli
4 dried shiitake mushrooms
1 tbsp groundnut oil
2 medium carrots, peeled and cut
  into fine matchsticks
125 g/4 oz mangetout, cut
  lengthways into fine strips
3 spring onions, trimmed
  and chopped
125 g/4 oz canned bamboo shoots,
  cut into fine matchsticks
1 cm/½ inch piece fresh root ginger,
  peeled and grated
1 tbsp light soy sauce
1 medium egg, separated
salt and freshly ground black pepper
20 spring roll wrappers, each about
  12.5 cm/5 inch square
vegetable oil for deep-frying
spring onion tassels, to garnish

1. Place the vermicelli in a bowl and pour over enough boiling water to cover. Leave to soak for 5 minutes or until softened, then drain. Cut into 7.5 cm/3 inch lengths. Soak the shiitake mushrooms in almost boiling water for 15 minutes, drain, discard the stalks and slice thinly.

2. Heat a wok or large frying pan, add the groundnut oil and when hot, add the carrots and stir-fry for 1 minute. Add the mangetout and spring onions and stir-fry for 2–3 minutes or until tender. Tip the vegetables into a bowl and leave to cool.

3. Stir the vermicelli and shiitake mushrooms into the cooled vegetables with the bamboo shoots, ginger, soy sauce and egg yolk. Season to taste with salt and pepper and mix thoroughly.

4. Brush the edges of a spring roll wrapper with a little beaten egg white. Spoon 2 teaspoons of the vegetable filling on to the wrapper, in a 7.5 cm/3 inch log shape 2.5 cm/1 inch from one edge. Fold the wrapper edge over the filling, then fold in the right and left sides. Brush the folded edges with more egg white and roll up neatly. Place on an oiled baking sheet, seam-side down and make the rest of the spring rolls.

5. Heat the oil in a heavy-based saucepan or deep-fat fryer to 180°C/350°F. Deep-fry the spring rolls, six at a time for 2–3 minutes, or until golden brown and crisp. Drain on absorbent kitchen paper and arrange on a warmed platter. Garnish with spring onion tassels and serve immediately.

1

2

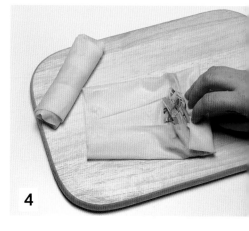

4

Sweetcorn Fritters

INGREDIENTS

Serves 4

4 tbsp groundnut oil
1 small onion, peeled and
  finely chopped
1 red chilli, deseeded and
  finely chopped
1 garlic clove, peeled and crushed
1 tsp ground coriander
325 g can sweetcorn
6 spring onions, trimmed and
  finely sliced
1 medium egg, lightly beaten
salt and freshly ground black pepper
3 tbsp plain flour
1 tsp baking powder
spring onion curls, to garnish
Thai-style chutney, to serve

HELPFUL HINT

To make a spring onion curl, trim off the root and some green top to leave 10 cm/4 inches. Make a 3 cm/1¼ inch cut down from the top, then make another cut at a right angle to the first cut. Continue making fine cuts. Soak the spring onions in iced water for 20 minutes and they open up and curl.

1 Heat 1 tablespoon of the groundnut oil in a frying pan, add the onion and cook gently for 7–8 minutes or until beginning to soften. Add the chilli, garlic and ground coriander and cook for 1 minute, stirring continuously. Remove from the heat.

2 Drain the sweetcorn and tip into a mixing bowl. Lightly mash with a potato masher to break down the corn a little. Add the cooked onion mixture to the bowl with the spring onions and beaten egg. Season to taste with salt and pepper, then stir to mix together. Sift the flour and baking powder over the mixture and stir in.

3 Heat 2 tablespoons of the groundnut oil in a large frying pan. Drop 4 or 5 heaped teaspoonfuls of the sweetcorn mixture into the pan, and using a fish slice or spatula, flatten each to make a 1 cm/½ inch thick fritter.

4 Fry the fritters for 3 minutes, or until golden brown on the underside, turn over and fry for a further 3 minutes, or until cooked through and crisp.

5 Remove the fritters from the pan and drain on absorbent kitchen paper. Keep warm while cooking the remaining fritters, adding a little more oil if needed. Garnish with spring onion curls and serve immediately with a Thai-style chutney.

1

2

4

Mixed Canapés

INGREDIENTS

Serves 12

For the stir-fried cheese canapés:

6 thick slices white bread

40 g/1½ oz butter, softened

75 g/3 oz mature Cheddar, cheese grated

75 g/3 oz blue cheese such as Stilton or Gorgonzola, crumbled

3 tbsp sunflower oil

For the spicy nuts:

25 g/1 oz unsalted butter

2 tbsp light olive oil

450 g/1 lb mixed unsalted nuts

1 tsp ground paprika

½ tsp ground cumin

½ tsp fine sea salt

sprigs of fresh coriander, to garnish

TASTY TIP

These canapés are perfect for serving at a buffet. Or you could halve the quantities and serve with drinks instead of a starter at an informal dinner party for four to six people.

1 For the cheese canapés, cut the crusts off the bread, then gently roll with a rolling pin to flatten slightly. Thinly spread with butter, then sprinkle over the mixed cheeses as evenly as possible.

2 Roll up each slice tightly, then cut into four slices, each about 2.5 cm/1 inch long. Heat the oil in a wok or large frying pan and stir-fry the cheese rolls in two batches, turning them all the time until golden brown and crisp. Drain on absorbent kitchen paper and serve warm or cold.

3 For the spicy nuts, melt the butter and oil in a wok, then add the nuts and stir-fry over a low heat for about 5 minutes, stirring all the time, or until they begin to colour.

4 Sprinkle the paprika and cumin over the nuts and continue stir-frying for a further 1–2 minutes, or until the nuts are golden brown.

5 Remove from the wok and drain on absorbent kitchen paper. Sprinkle with the salt, garnish with sprigs of fresh coriander and serve hot or cold. If serving cold, store both the cheese canapés and the spicy nuts in airtight containers.

Wild Rice Dolmades

INGREDIENTS

Serves 4–6

6 tbsp olive oil

25 g/1 oz pine nuts

175 g/6 oz mushrooms, wiped
  and finely chopped

4 spring onions, trimmed and
  finely chopped

1 garlic clove, peeled and crushed

50 g/2 oz cooked wild rice

2 tsp freshly chopped dill

2 tsp freshly chopped mint

salt and freshly ground black pepper

16–24 prepared medium vine leaves

about 300 ml/½ pint vegetable stock

To garnish:
lemon wedges

sprigs of fresh dill

HELPFUL HINT

Fresh vine leaves are available in early summer and should be blanched for 2–3 minutes in boiling water. Vine leaves preserved in brine can be found all year round in supermarkets – soak in warm water for 20 minutes before using.

1 Heat 1 tbsp of the oil in a frying pan and gently cook the pine nuts for 2–3 minutes, stirring frequently, until golden. Remove from the pan and reserve.

2 Add 1½ tablespoons of oil to the pan and gently cook the mushrooms, spring onions and garlic for 7–8 minutes until very soft. Stir in the rice, herbs, salt and pepper.

3 Put a heaped teaspoon of stuffing in the centre of each leaf (if the leaves are small, put two together, overlapping slightly). Fold over the stalk end, then the sides and roll up to make a neat parcel. Continue until all the stuffing is used.

4 Arrange the stuffed vine leaves close together seam-side down in a large saucepan, drizzling each with a little of the remaining oil – there will be several layers. Pour over just enough stock to cover.

5 Put an inverted plate over the dolmades to stop them unrolling during cooking. Bring to the boil, then simmer very gently for 3 minutes. Cool in the saucepan.

6 Transfer the dolmades to a serving dish. Cover and chill in the refrigerator before serving. Sprinkle with the pine nuts and garnish with lemon and dill. Serve.

Potato Skins

INGREDIENTS

Serves 4

4 large baking potatoes
2 tbsp olive oil
2 tsp paprika
125 g/4 oz pancetta, roughly chopped
6 tbsp double cream
125 g/4 oz Gorgonzola cheese
1 tbsp freshly chopped parsley

To serve:
mayonnaise
sweet chilli dipping sauce
tossed green salad

FOOD FACT

A popular, well-known Italian cheese, Gorgonzola was first made over 1,100 years ago in the village of the same name near Milan. Now mostly produced in Lombardy, it is made from pasteurised cows' milk and allowed to ripen for at least 3 months, giving it a rich but not overpowering flavour. Unlike most blue cheeses, it should have a greater concentration of veining towards the centre of the cheese.

1 Preheat the oven to 200°C/400°F/Gas Mark 6. Scrub the potatoes, then prick a few times with a fork or skewer and place directly on the top shelf of the oven. Bake in the preheated oven for at least 1 hour, or until tender. The potatoes are cooked when they yield gently to the pressure of your hand.

2 Set the potatoes aside until cool enough to handle, then cut in half and scoop the flesh into a bowl and reserve. Preheat the grill and line the grill rack with tinfoil.

3 Mix together the oil and the paprika and use half to brush the outside of the potato skins. Place on the grill rack under the preheated hot grill and cook for 5 minutes, or until crisp, turning as necessary.

4 Heat the remaining paprika-flavoured oil and gently fry the pancetta until crisp. Add to the potato flesh along with the cream, Gorgonzola cheese and parsley. Halve the potato skins and fill with the Gorgonzola filling. Return to the oven for a further 15 minutes to heat through. Sprinkle with a little more paprika and serve immediately with mayonnaise, sweet chilli sauce and a green salad.

2

3

4

Sweet Potato Crisps with Mango Salsa

INGREDIENTS

Serves 6

For the salsa:
1 large mango, peeled, stoned and
 cut into small cubes
8 cherry tomatoes, quartered
½ cucumber, peeled if preferred and
 finely diced
1 red onion, peeled and finely chopped
pinch of sugar
1 red chilli, deseeded and
 finely chopped
2 tbsp rice vinegar
2 tbsp olive oil
grated rind and juice of 1 lime

450 g/1 lb sweet potatoes, peeled
 and thinly sliced
vegetable oil, for deep frying
sea salt
2 tbsp freshly chopped mint

1 To make the salsa, mix the mango with the tomatoes, cucumber and onion. Add the sugar, chilli, vinegar, oil and the lime rind and juice. Mix together thoroughly, cover and leave for 45–50 minutes.

2 Soak the potatoes in cold water for 40 minutes to remove as much of the excess starch as possible. Drain and dry thoroughly in a clean tea towel, or absorbent kitchen paper.

3 Heat the oil to 190°C/375°F in a deep fryer. When at the correct temperature, place half the potatoes in the frying basket, then carefully lower the potatoes into the hot oil and cook for 4–5 minutes, or until they are golden brown, shaking the basket every minute so that they do not stick together.

4 Drain the potato crisps on absorbent kitchen paper, sprinkle with sea salt and place under a preheated moderate grill for a few seconds to dry out. Repeat with the remaining potatoes. Stir the mint into the salsa and serve with the potato crisps.

1

3

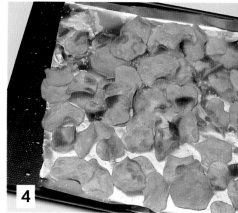

4

Stuffed Tomatoes with Grilled Polenta

INGREDIENTS

Serves 4

For the polenta:
300 ml/½ pint vegetable stock
salt and freshly ground black pepper
50 g/2 oz quick-cook polenta
15 g/½ oz butter

For the stuffed tomatoes:
4 large tomatoes
1 tbsp olive oil
1 garlic clove, peeled and crushed
1 bunch spring onions, trimmed and
  finely chopped
2 tbsp freshly chopped parsley
2 tbsp freshly chopped basil
2 slices Parma ham, cut into
  thin slivers
50 g/2 oz fresh white breadcrumbs
snipped chives, to garnish

1 Preheat grill just before cooking. To make the polenta, pour the stock into a saucepan. Add a pinch of salt and bring to the boil. Pour in the polenta in a fine stream, stirring all the time. Simmer for about 15 minutes, or until very thick. Stir in the butter and add a little pepper. Turn the polenta out on to a chopping board and spread to a thickness of just over 1 cm/½ inch. Cool, cover with clingfilm and chill in the refrigerator for 30 minutes.

2 To make the stuffed tomatoes, cut the tomatoes in half then scoop out the seeds and press through a fine sieve to extract the juices. Season the insides of the tomatoes with salt and pepper and reserve.

3 Heat the olive oil in a saucepan and gently fry the garlic and spring onions for 3 minutes. Add the tomatoes' juices, bubble for 3–4 minutes, until most of the liquid has evaporated. Stir in the herbs, Parma ham and a little black pepper with half the breadcrumbs. Spoon into the hollowed out tomatoes and reserve.

4 Cut the polenta into 5 cm/2 inch squares, then cut each in half diagonally to make triangles. Put the triangles on a piece of tinfoil on the grill rack and grill for 4–5 minutes on each side, until golden. Cover and keep warm.

5 Grill the tomatoes under a medium-hot grill for about 4 minutes – any exposed Parma ham will become crisp. Sprinkle with the remaining breadcrumbs and grill for 1–2 minutes, or until the breadcrumbs are golden brown. Garnish with snipped chives and serve immediately with the grilled polenta.

1

3

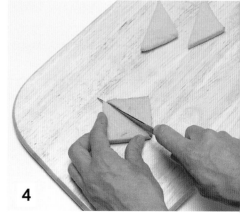

4

Mixed Salad with Anchovy Dressing & Ciabatta Croûtons

INGREDIENTS

Serves 4

1 small head endive
1 small head chicory
1 fennel bulb
400 g can artichokes, drained
 and rinsed
½ cucumber
125 g/4 oz cherry tomatoes
75 g/3 oz black olives

For the anchovy dressing:

50 g can anchovy fillets
1 tsp Dijon mustard
1 small garlic clove, peeled
 and crushed
4 tbsp olive oil
1 tbsp lemon juice
freshly ground black pepper

For the ciabatta croûtons:

2 thick slices ciabatta bread
2 tbsp olive oil

1. Divide the endive and chicory into leaves and reserve some of the larger ones. Arrange the smaller leaves in a wide salad bowl.

2. Cut the fennel bulb in half from the stalk to the root end, then cut across in fine slices. Quarter the artichokes, then quarter and slice the cucumber and halve the tomatoes. Add to the salad bowl with the olives.

3. To make the dressing, drain the anchovies and put in a blender with the mustard, garlic, olive oil, lemon juice, 2 tablespoons of hot water and black pepper. Whizz together until smooth and thickened.

4. To make the croûtons, cut the bread into 1 cm/½ inch cubes. Heat the oil in a frying pan, add the bread cubes and fry for 3 minutes, turning frequently until golden. Remove and drain on absorbent kitchen paper.

5. Drizzle half the anchovy dressing over the prepared salad and toss to coat. Arrange the reserved endive and chicory leaves around the edge, then drizzle over the remaining dressing. Scatter over the croûtons and serve immediately.

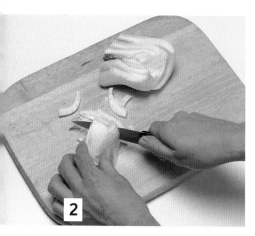

2

3

4

Tortellini, Cherry Tomato & Mozzarella Skewers

INGREDIENTS

Serves 6

250 g/9 oz mixed green and plain
   cheese or vegetable-filled
   fresh tortellini
150 ml/¼ pint extra virgin olive oil
2 garlic cloves, peeled and crushed
pinch dried thyme or basil
salt and freshly ground black pepper
225 g/8 oz cherry tomatoes
450 g/1 lb mozzarella, cut into
   2.5 cm/1 inch cubes
basil leaves, to garnish
dressed salad leaves, to serve

HELPFUL HINT

These skewers make an ideal starter for a barbecue. If using wooden skewers for this recipe, soak them in cold water for at least 30 minutes before cooking to prevent them scorching under the grill. The tips of the skewers may be protected with small pieces of foil.

1 Preheat the grill and line a grill pan with tinfoil, just before cooking. Bring a large pan of lightly salted water to a rolling boil. Add the tortellini and cook according to the packet instructions, or until 'al dente'. Drain, rinse under cold running water, drain again and toss with 2 tablespoons of the olive oil and reserve.

2 Pour the remaining olive oil into a small bowl. Add the crushed garlic and thyme or basil, then blend well. Season to taste with salt and black pepper and reserve.

3 To assemble the skewers, thread the tortellini alternately with the cherry tomatoes and cubes of mozzarella. Arrange the skewers on the grill pan and brush generously on all sides with the olive oil mixture.

4 Cook the skewers under the preheated grill for about 5 minutes, or until they begin to turn golden, turning them halfway through cooking. Arrange two skewers on each plate and garnish with a few basil leaves. Serve immediately with dressed salad leaves.

2

3

3

Pasta Triangles with Pesto & Walnut Dressing

INGREDIENTS

Serves 6

450 g/1 lb fresh egg lasagne
4 tbsp ricotta cheese
4 tbsp pesto
125 g/4 oz walnuts
1 slice white bread, crusts removed
150 ml/¼ pint soured cream
75 g/3 oz mascarpone cheese
25 g/1 oz pecorino cheese, grated
salt and freshly ground black pepper
1 tbsp olive oil
sprig of dill or freshly chopped basil
  or parsley, to garnish
tomato and cucumber salad, to serve

TASTY TIP

For the salad, arrange overlapping thin slices of cucumber and beef and plum tomatoes on a large plate. Drizzle over a dressing made with 1 tsp Dijon mustard, 4 tbsp extra virgin olive oil, 1 tbsp lemon juice and a pinch each of caster sugar, salt and pepper. Leave at room temperature for 15 minutes before serving.

1 Preheat the grill to high. Cut the lasagne sheets in half, then into triangles and reserve. Mix the pesto and ricotta cheese together and warm gently in a pan.

2 Toast the walnuts under the preheated grill until golden. Rub off the papery skins. Place the nuts in a food processor with the bread and grind finely.

3 Mix the soured cream with the mascarpone cheese in a bowl. Add the ground walnuts and grated pecorino cheese and season to taste with salt and pepper. Whisk in the olive oil. Pour into a pan and warm gently.

4 Bring a large pan of lightly salted water to a rolling boil. Add the pasta triangles and cook, according to the packet instructions, for about 3–4 minutes or until 'al dente'.

5 Drain the pasta thoroughly and arrange a few triangles on each serving plate. Top each one with a spoonful of the pesto mixture then place another triangle on top. Continue to layer the pasta and pesto mixture, then spoon a little of the walnut sauce on top of each stack. Garnish with dill, basil or parsley and serve immediately with a freshly dressed tomato and cucumber salad.

1

2

3

Mozzarella Frittata with Tomato & Basil Salad

INGREDIENTS

Serves 4

For the salad:

6 ripe but firm tomatoes
2 tbsp fresh basil leaves
2 tbsp olive oil
1 tbsp fresh lemon juice
1 tsp caster sugar
freshly ground black pepper

For the frittata:

7 medium eggs, beaten
salt
300 g/11 oz mozzarella cheese
2 spring onions, trimmed and
  finely chopped
2 tbsp olive oil
warm crusty bread, to serve

HELPFUL HINT

Fresh mozzarella is sold in packets and is usually surrounded by a light brine. After grating the cheese, firmly press between layers of absorbent kitchen paper to remove any excess water which might leak out during cooking.

1   To make the tomato and basil salad, slice the tomatoes very thinly, tear up the basil leaves and sprinkle over. Make the dressing by whisking the olive oil, lemon juice and sugar together well. Season with black pepper before drizzling the dressing over the salad.

2   To make the frittata, preheat the grill to a high heat, just before beginning to cook. Place the eggs in a large bowl with plenty of salt and whisk. Grate the mozzarella and stir into the egg with the finely chopped spring onions.

3   Heat the oil in a large, non-stick frying pan and pour in the egg mixture, stirring with a wooden spoon to spread the ingredients evenly over the pan.

4   Cook for 5–8 minutes, until the frittata is golden brown and firm on the underside. Place the whole pan under the preheated grill and cook for about 4–5 minutes, or until the top is golden brown. Slide the frittata on to a serving plate, cut into six large wedges and serve immediately with the tomato and basil salad and plenty of warm crusty bread.

2

3

4

Stilton, Tomato & Courgette Quiche

INGREDIENTS

Serves 4

1 quantity shortcrust pastry
  (see page 28)
25 g/1 oz butter
1 onion, peeled and finely chopped
1 courgette, trimmed and sliced
125 g/4 oz Stilton cheese, crumbled
6 cherry tomatoes, halved
2 large eggs, beaten
200 ml tub crème fraîche
salt and freshly ground black pepper

FOOD FACT

Stilton is a very traditional British cheese which often makes an appearance on the cheese board or served with a ploughman's lunch. It gets much of its full pungent flavour from its veins (created from the steel wires which are inserted into the cheese during the maturing process). It is worth looking for a piece of Stilton with lots of veins that has been matured for longer.

1. Preheat the oven to 190°C/375°F/Gas Mark 5. On a lightly floured surface, roll out the pastry and use to line an 18 cm/7 inch lightly oiled quiche or flan tin, trimming any excess pastry with a knife.

2. Prick the base all over with a fork and bake blind in the preheated oven for 15 minutes. Remove the pastry from the oven and brush with a little of the beaten egg. Return to the oven for a further 5 minutes.

3. Heat the butter in a frying pan and gently fry the onion and courgette for about 4 minutes until soft and starting to brown. Transfer into the pastry case.

4. Sprinkle the Stilton over evenly and top with the halved cherry tomatoes. Beat together the eggs and crème fraîche and season to taste with salt and pepper.

5. Pour the filling into the pastry case and bake in the oven for 35–40 minutes, or until the filling is golden brown and set in the centre. Serve the quiche hot or cold.

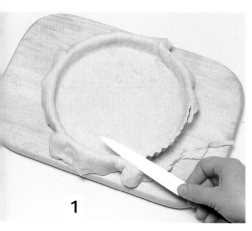
1

3

4

Garlic Wild Mushroom Galettes

INGREDIENTS

Serves 6

225 g/8 oz shop-bought flaky pastry
1 onion, peeled
1 red chilli, deseeded
2 garlic cloves, peeled
275 g/10 oz mixed mushrooms
   e.g. oyster, chestnuts, morels,
   ceps and chanterelles
25 g/1 oz butter
2 tbsp freshly chopped parsley
125 g/4 oz mozzarella cheese, sliced

To serve:
cherry tomatoes
mixed green salad leaves

HELPFUL HINT

Many supermarkets now stock a variety of wild mushrooms, all of which can be used in this recipe. It is important to maintain as much of the flavour of the mushrooms as possible, so do not peel mushrooms unless they appear old or tough. Either rinse lightly if covered with small pieces of soil or wipe well, trim the stalks and use.

1   Preheat the oven to 220°C/425°F/Gas Mark 7. On a lightly floured surface roll out the chilled pastry very thinly.

2   Cut out 6 x 15 cm/6 inch circles and place on a lightly oiled baking sheet.

3   Thinly slice the onion, then divide into rings and reserve.

4   Thinly slice the chilli and slice the garlic into wafer-thin slivers. Add to the onions and reserve.

5   Wipe or lightly rinse the mushrooms. Half or quarter any large mushrooms and keep the small ones whole.

6   Heat the butter in a frying pan and sauté the onion, chilli and garlic gently for about 3 minutes. Add the mushrooms and cook for about 5 minutes, or until beginning to soften.

7   Stir the parsley into the mushroom mixture and drain off any excess liquid.

8   Pile the mushroom mixture on to the pastry circles within 5 mm/¼ inches of the edge. Arrange the sliced mozzarella cheese on top.

9   Bake in the preheated oven for 12–15 minutes, or until golden brown and serve with the tomatoes and salad.

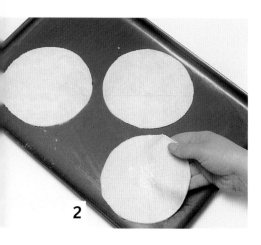

2

5

8

Fennel & Caramelised Shallot Tartlets

INGREDIENTS

Serves 6

Cheese pastry:

176 g/6 oz plain white flour
75 g/3 oz slightly salted butter
50 g/2 oz Gruyère cheese, grated
1 small egg yolk

For the filling:

2 tbsp olive oil
225 g/8 oz shallots, peeled
  and halved
1 fennel bulb, trimmed and sliced
1 tsp soft brown sugar
1 medium egg
150 ml/¼ pint double cream
salt and freshly ground black pepper
25 g/1 oz Gruyère cheese, grated
½ tsp ground cinnamon
mixed salad leaves, to serve

TASTY TIP

Fennel has a very aromatic, almost aniseed flavour, which works particularly well with the sweet shallots and the cheese in this dish. Try adding a grating of nutmeg in step 5, as this compliments the creamy cheese filling.

1 Preheat the oven to 200°C/400°F/Gas Mark 6. Sift the flour into a bowl, then rub in the butter, using the fingertips. Stir in the cheese, then add the egg yolk with about 2 tablespoons of cold water. Mix to a firm dough, then knead lightly. Wrap in clingfilm and chill in the refrigerator for 30 minutes.

2 Roll out the pastry on a lightly floured surface and use to line 6 x 10 cm/4 inch individual flan tins or patty tins which are about 2 cm/³⁄₄ inch deep.

3 Line the pastry cases with greaseproof paper and fill with baking beans or rice. Bake blind in the preheated oven for about 10 minutes, then remove the paper and beans.

4 Heat the oil in a frying pan, add the shallots and fennel and fry gently for 5 minutes. Sprinkle with the sugar and cook for a further 10 minutes, stirring occasionally until lightly caramelised. Reserve until cooled.

5 Beat together the egg and cream and season to taste with salt and pepper. Divide the shallot mixture between the pastry cases. Pour over the egg mixture and sprinkle with the cheese and cinnamon. Bake for 20 minutes, until golden and set. Serve with the salad leaves.

3

4

5

Spinach, Pine Nut & Mascarpone Pizza

INGREDIENTS

Serves 2–4

Basic pizza dough:

225 g/8 oz strong plain flour

½ tsp salt

¼ tsp quick-acting dried yeast

150 ml/¼ pint warm water

1 tbsp extra virgin olive oil

For the topping:

3 tbsp olive oil

1 large red onion, peeled
   and chopped

2 garlic cloves, peeled and
   finely sliced

450 g/1 lb frozen spinach, thawed
   and drained

salt and freshly ground black pepper

3 tbsp passata

125 g/4 oz mascarpone cheese

1 tbsp toasted pine nuts

1 Preheat the oven to 220°C/425°F/Gas Mark 7. Sift the flour and salt into a bowl and stir in the yeast. Make a well in the centre and gradually add the water and oil to form soft dough.

2 Knead the dough on a floured surface for about 5 minutes until smooth and elastic. Place in a lightly oiled bowl and cover with clingfilm. Leave to rise in a warm place for 1 hour.

3 Knock the pizza dough with your fist a few times, shape and roll out thinly on a lightly floured board. Place on a lightly floured baking sheet and lift the edge to make a little rim. Place another baking sheet into the preheated oven to heat up.

4 Heat half the oil in a frying pan and gently fry the onion and garlic until soft and starting to change colour.

5 Squeeze out any excess water from the spinach and finely chop. Add to the onion and garlic with the remaining olive oil. Season to taste with salt and pepper.

6 Spread the passata on the pizza dough and top with the spinach mixture. Mix the mascarpone with the pine nuts and dot over the pizza.

7 Slide the pizza on to the hot baking sheet and bake for 15–20 minutes. Transfer to a large plate and serve immediately.

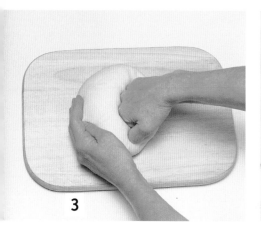

3

3

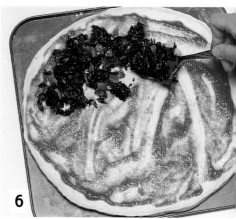

6

Roquefort, Parma & Rocket Pizza

INGREDIENTS

Serves 2–4

1 quantity pizza dough (see page 86)

Basic tomato sauce:
400 g can chopped tomatoes
2 garlic cloves, peeled and crushed
grated rind of ½ lime
2 tbsp extra virgin olive oil
2 tbsp freshly chopped basil
½ tsp sugar
salt and freshly ground black pepper

For the topping:
125 g/4 oz Roquefort cheese, cut into
  chunks
6 slices Parma ham
50 g/2 oz rocket leaves, rinsed
1 tbsp extra virgin olive oil
50 g/2 oz Parmesan cheese,
  freshly shaved

1 Preheat the oven to 220°C/425°F/Gas Mark 7. Roll the pizza dough out on a lightly floured board to form a 25.5 cm/10 inch round.

2 Lightly cover the dough and reserve while making the sauce. Place a baking sheet in the preheated oven to heat up.

3 Place all of the tomato sauce ingredients in a large heavy-based saucepan and slowly bring to the boil.

4 Cover and simmer for 15 minutes, uncover and cook for a further 10 minutes until the sauce has thickened and reduced by half.

5 Spoon the tomato sauce over the shaped pizza dough. Place on the hot baking sheet and bake for 10 minutes.

6 Remove the pizza from the oven and top with the Roquefort and Parma ham, then bake for a further 10 minutes.

7 Toss the rocket in the olive oil and pile on to the pizza. Sprinkle with the Parmesan cheese and serve immediately.

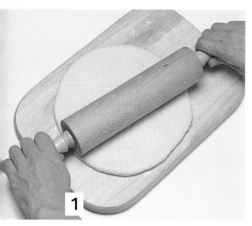
1

3

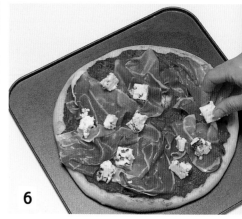
6

Three Tomato Pizza

INGREDIENTS

Serves 2–4

1 quantity pizza dough (see page 86)
3 plum tomatoes
8 cherry tomatoes
6 sun-dried tomatoes
pinch of sea salt
1 tbsp freshly chopped basil
2 tbsp extra virgin olive oil
125 g/4 oz buffalo mozzarella
  cheese, sliced
freshly ground black pepper
fresh basil leaves, to garnish

FOOD FACT

Buffalo mozzarella is considered the king of mozzarellas. It uses buffalo milk, which results in the cheese tasting extremely mild and creamy. A good mozzarella should come in liquid to keep it moist and should tear easily into chunks.

1   Preheat the oven to 220°C/425°F/Gas Mark 7. Place a baking sheet into the oven to heat up.

2   Divide the prepared pizza dough into four equal pieces.

3   Roll out one piece on a lightly floured board to form a 20.5 cm/8 inch round.

4   Lightly cover the three remaining pieces of dough with clingfilm.

5   Roll out the other three pieces into rounds, one at a time. While rolling out any piece of dough, keep the others covered with the clingfilm.

6   Slice the plum tomatoes, halve the cherry tomatoes and chop the sun-dried tomatoes into small pieces.

7   Place a few pieces of each type of tomato on each pizza base then season to taste with the sea salt.

8   Sprinkle with the chopped basil and drizzle with the olive oil. Place a few slices of mozzarella on each pizza and season with black pepper.

9   Transfer the pizza on to the heated baking sheet and cook for 15–20 minutes, or until the cheese is golden brown and bubbling. Garnish with the basil leaves and serve immediately.

3

7

8

Tomato & Courgette Herb Tart

INGREDIENTS

Serves 4

4 tbsp olive oil
1 onion, peeled and finely chopped
3 garlic cloves, peeled and crushed
400 g/14 oz prepared puff pastry,
   thawed if frozen
1 small egg, beaten
2 tbsp freshly chopped rosemary
2 tbsp freshly chopped parsley
175 g/6 oz rindless fresh
   soft goats' cheese
4 ripe plum tomatoes, sliced
1 medium courgette, trimmed
   and sliced
thyme sprigs, to garnish

1 Preheat the oven to 230°C/450°F/Gas Mark 8. Heat 2 tablespoons of the oil in a large frying pan.

2 Fry the onion and garlic for about 4 minutes until softened and reserve.

3 Roll out the pastry on a lightly floured surface, and cut out a 30.5 cm/12 inch circle.

4 Brush the pastry with a little beaten egg, then prick all over with a fork.

5 Transfer on to a dampened baking sheet and bake in the preheated oven for 10 minutes.

6 Turn the pastry over and brush with a little more egg. Bake for 5 more minutes, then remove from the oven.

7 Mix together the onion, garlic and herbs with the goats' cheese and spread over the pastry.

8 Arrange the tomatoes and courgettes over the goats' cheese and drizzle with the remaining oil.

9 Bake for 20–25 minutes, or until the pastry is golden brown and the topping bubbling. Garnish with the thyme sprigs and serve immediately.

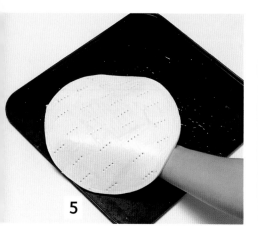

5

7

8

Red Pepper & Basil Tart

INGREDIENTS

Serves 4–6

For the olive pastry:
225 g/8 oz plain flour
pinch of salt
50 g/2 oz pitted black olives,
 finely chopped
1 medium egg, lightly beaten,
 plus 1 egg yolk
3 tbsp olive oil

For the filling:
2 large red peppers, quartered
and deseeded
175 g/6 oz mascarpone cheese
4 tbsp milk
2 medium eggs
3 tbsp freshly chopped basil
salt and freshly ground black pepper
sprig of fresh basil, to garnish
mixed salad, to serve

1 Preheat oven to 200°C/400°F/Gas Mark 6, 15 minutes before cooking. Sift the flour and salt into a bowl. Make a well in the centre. Stir together the egg, oil and 1 tablespoon of tepid water. Add to the dry ingredients, drop in the olives and mix to a dough. Knead on a lightly floured surface for a few seconds until smooth, then wrap in clingfilm and chill in the refrigerator for 30 minutes.

2 Roll out the pastry and use to line a 23 cm/9 inch loose-bottomed fluted flan tin. Lightly prick the base with a fork. Cover and chill in the refrigerator for 20 minutes.

3 Cook the peppers under a hot grill for 10 minutes, or until the skins are blackened and blistered. Put the peppers in a plastic bag, cool for 10 minutes, then remove the skin and slice.

4 Line the pastry case with tinfoil or greaseproof paper weighed down with baking beans and bake in the preheated oven for 10 minutes. Remove the tinfoil and beans and bake for a further 5 minutes. Reduce the oven temperature to 180°C/350°F/Gas Mark 4.

5 Beat the mascarpone cheese until smooth. Gradually add the milk and eggs. Stir in the peppers, basil and season to taste with salt and pepper. Spoon into the flan case and bake for 25–30 minutes, or until lightly set. Garnish with a sprig of fresh basil and serve immediately with a mixed salad.

1

3

5

Olive & Feta Parcels

INGREDIENTS

Makes 30

1 small red pepper
1 small yellow pepper
125 g/4 oz assorted marinated green
  and black olives
125 g/4 oz feta cheese
2 tbsp pine nuts, lightly toasted
6 sheets filo pastry
3 tbsp olive oil
sour cream and chive dip, to serve

HELPFUL HINT

Feta is generally made from goats' milk and has quite a salty taste. To make the cheese less salty simply soak it in milk, then drain before eating.

1   Preheat the oven to 180°C/350°F/Gas Mark 4. Preheat the grill, then line the grill rack with tinfoil.

2   Cut the peppers into quarters and remove the seeds. Place skin side up on the foil-lined grill rack and cook under the preheated grill for 10 minutes, turning occasionally until the skins begin to blacken.

3   Place the peppers in a polythene bag and leave until cool enough to handle, then skin and thinly slice.

4   Chop the olives and cut the feta cheese into small cubes. Mix together the olives, feta, sliced peppers and pine nuts.

5   Cut 1 sheet of filo pastry in half then brush with a little of the oil. Place a spoonful of the olive and feta mix about one-third of the way up the pastry.

6   Fold over the pastry and wrap to form a square parcel encasing the filling completely.

7   Place this parcel in the centre of the second half of the pastry sheet. Brush the edges lightly with a little oil, bring up the corners to meet in the centre and twist them loosely to form a purse.

8   Brush with a little more oil and repeat with the remaining filo pastry and filling.

9   Place the parcels on a lightly oiled baking sheet and bake in the preheated oven for 10–15 minutes, or until crisp and golden brown. Serve with the dip.

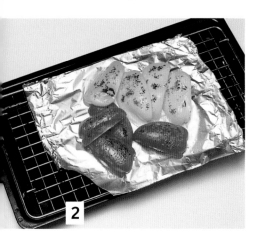

2

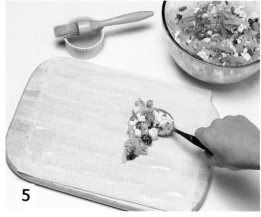

5

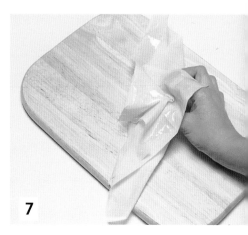

7

Rosemary & Olive Focaccia

INGREDIENTS

Makes 2 loaves

700 g/1½ lb strong white flour
pinch of salt
pinch of caster sugar
7 g/ ¼ oz sachet easy-blend
   dried yeast
2 tsp freshly chopped rosemary
450 ml/¾ pint warm water
3 tbsp olive oil
75 g/3 oz pitted black olives,
   roughly chopped
sprigs of rosemary, to garnish

To finish:

3 tbsp olive oil
coarse sea salt
freshly ground black pepper

TASTY TIP

As a variation to the rosemary used in this bread, replace with a little chopped sun-dried tomatoes. Knead the tomatoes into the dough along with the olives in step 3, then before baking drizzle with the oil and replace the salt with some grated mozzarella cheese.

1 Preheat the oven to 200°C/400°F/Gas Mark 6 15 minutes before baking. Sift the flour, salt and sugar into a large bowl. Stir in the yeast and rosemary. Make a well in the centre.

2 Pour in the warm water and the oil and mix to a soft dough. Turn out on to a lightly floured surface and knead for about 10 minutes, until smooth and elastic.

3 Pat the olives dry on kitchen paper, then gently knead into the dough. Put in an oiled bowl, cover with clingfilm and leave to rise in a warm place for 1½ hours, or until it has doubled in size.

4 Turn out the dough and knead again for a minute or two. Divide in half and roll out each piece to a 25.5 cm/10 inch circle.

5 Transfer to oiled baking sheets, cover with oiled clingfilm and leave to rise for 30 minutes.

6 Using the fingertips, make deep dimples all over the the dough. Drizzle with the oil and sprinkle with sea salt.

7 Bake in the preheated oven for 20–25 minutes, or until risen and golden. Cool on a wire rack and garnish with sprigs of rosemary. Grind over a little black pepper before serving.

3

4

6

Cheese-crusted Potato Scones

INGREDIENTS

Makes 6

200 g/7 oz self-raising flour
25 g/1 oz wholemeal flour
½ tsp salt
1½ tsp baking powder
25 g/1 oz butter, cubed
5 tbsp milk
175 g/6 oz cold mashed potato
freshly ground black pepper

To finish:

2 tbsp milk
40 g/1½ oz mature Cheddar cheese, finely grated
paprika pepper, to dust
sprig of basil, to garnis

FOOD FACT

The scone supposedly acquired its name from the Stone of Destiny (or Scone) in Scotland where Scottish Kings were once crowned.

1 Preheat the oven to 220°C/425°F/Gas Mark 7, 15 minutes before baking. Sift the flours, salt and baking powder into a large bowl. Rub in the butter until the mixture resembles fine breadcrumbs.

2 Stir 4 tablespoons of the milk into the mashed potato and season with black pepper.

3 Add the dry ingredients to the potato mixture, mixing together with a fork and adding the remaining 1 tablespoon of milk if needed.

4 Knead the dough on a lightly floured surface for a few seconds until smooth. Roll out to a 15 cm/6 inch round and transfer to an oiled baking sheet.

5 Mark the scone round into six wedges, cutting about halfway through with a small sharp knife.

6 Brush with milk, then sprinkle with the cheese and a faint dusting of paprika.

7 Bake on the middle shelf of the preheated oven for 15 minutes, or until well risen and golden brown.

8 Transfer to a wire rack and leave to cool for 5 minutes before breaking into wedges.

9 Serve warm or leave to cool completely. Once cool store the scones in an airtight tin. Garnish with a sprig of basil and serve split and buttered.

Scallop & Potato Gratin

INGREDIENTS

Serves 4

8 fresh scallops in their shells, cleaned
4 tbsp white wine
salt and freshly ground black pepper
50 g/2 oz butter
3 tbsp plain flour
2 tbsp single cream
50 g/2 oz Cheddar cheese, grated
450 g/1 lb potatoes, peeled and cut
   into chunks
1 tbsp milk

1 Preheat the oven to 220°C/425°F/Gas Mark 7. Clean four scallop shells to use as serving dishes and reserve. Place the scallops in a small saucepan with the wine, 150 ml/¼ pint water and salt and pepper. Cover and simmer very gently for 5 minutes, or until just tender. Remove with a slotted spoon and cut each scallop into three pieces. Reserve the cooking juices.

2 Melt 25 g/1 oz of the butter in a saucepan, stir in the flour and cook for 1 minute, stirring, then gradually whisk in the reserved cooking juices. Simmer, stirring, for 3–4 minutes until the sauce has thickened. Season to taste with salt and pepper. Remove from the heat and stir in the cream and 25 g/1 oz of the grated cheese. Fold in the scallops.

3 Boil the potatoes in lightly salted water until tender, then mash with the remaining butter and milk. Spoon or pipe the mashed potato around the edges of the cleaned scallop shells.

4 Divide the scallop mixture between the four shells, placing the mixture neatly in the centre. Sprinkle with the remaining grated cheese and bake in the preheated oven for about 10–15 minutes until golden brown and bubbling. Serve immediately.

1

2

4

Salmon & Filo Parcels

INGREDIENTS

Serves 4

1 tbsp sunflower oil
1 bunch of spring onions, trimmed
   and finely chopped
1 tsp paprika
175 g/6 oz long-grain white rice
300 ml/½ pint fish stock
salt and freshly ground black pepper
450 g/1 lb salmon fillet, cubed
1 tbsp freshly chopped parsley
grated rind and juice of 1 lemon
150 g/5 oz rocket
150 g/5 oz spinach
12 sheets filo pastry
50 g/2 oz butter, melted

1 Preheat the oven to 200°C/400°F/Gas Mark 6. Heat the oil in a small frying pan and gently cook the spring onions for 2 minutes. Stir in the paprika and continue to cook for 1 minute, then remove from the heat and reserve.

2 Put the rice in a sieve and rinse under cold running water until the water runs clear; drain. Put the rice and stock in a saucepan, bring to the boil, then cover and simmer for 10 minutes, or until the liquid is absorbed and the rice is tender. Add the spring onion mixture and fork through. Season to taste with salt and pepper, then leave to cool.

3 In a non-metallic bowl, mix together the salmon, parsley, lemon rind and juice and salt and pepper. Reserve.

4 Blanch the rocket and spinach for 30 seconds in a large saucepan of boiling water, or until just wilted. Drain well in a colander and refresh in plenty of cold water, then squeeze out as much moisture as possible.

5 Brush three sheets of filo pastry with melted butter and lay them on top of one another. Take a quarter of the rice mixture and arrange it in an oblong in the centre of the pastry. On top of this place a quarter of the salmon followed by a quarter of the rocket and spinach.

6 Draw up the pastry around the filling and twist at the top to create a parcel. Repeat with the remaining pastry and filling until you have four parcels. Brush with the remaining butter.

7 Place the parcels on a lightly oiled baking tray and cook in the preheated oven for 20 minutes, or until golden brown and cooked. Serve immediately.

1

2

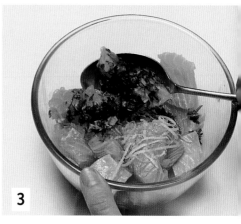

3

Thai Green Fragrant Mussels

INGREDIENTS

Serves 4

2 kg/4½ lb fresh mussels

4 tbsp olive oil

2 garlic cloves, peeled and
finely sliced

3 tbsp fresh root ginger, peeled
and finely sliced

3 lemon grass stalks, outer leaves
discarded and finely sliced

1–3 red or green chillies, deseeded
and chopped

1 green pepper, deseeded and diced

5 spring onions, trimmed and
finely sliced

3 tbsp freshly chopped coriander

1 tbsp sesame oil

juice of 3 limes

400 ml can coconut milk

warm crusty bread, to serve

1 Scrub the mussels under cold running water, removing any barnacles and beards. Discard any that have broken or damaged shells or are opened and do not close when tapped gently.

2 Heat a wok or large frying pan, add the oil and when hot, add the mussels. Shake gently and cook for 1 minute, then add the garlic, ginger, sliced lemon grass, chillies, green pepper, spring onions, 2 tablespoons of the chopped coriander and the sesame oil.

3 Stir-fry over a medium heat for 3–4 minutes, or until the mussels are cooked and have opened. Discard any mussels that remain unopened.

4 Pour the lime juice with the coconut milk into the wok and bring to the boil. Tip the mussels and the cooking liquor into warmed individual bowls. Sprinkle with the remaining chopped coriander and serve immediately with warm crusty bread.

1

2

4

Ginger Lobster

INGREDIENTS

Serves 4

1 celery stalk, trimmed and
  finely chopped
1 onion, peeled and chopped
1 small leek, trimmed and chopped
10 black peppercorns
1 x 550 g/1¼ lb live lobster
25 g/1 oz butter
75 g/3 oz raw prawns, peeled and
  finely chopped
6 tbsp fish stock
50 g/2 oz fresh root ginger, peeled
  and cut into matchsticks
2 shallots, peeled and finely chopped
4 shiitake mushrooms, wiped and
  finely chopped
1 tsp green peppercorns, drained
  and crushed
2 tbsp oyster sauce
freshly ground black pepper
¼ tsp cornflour
sprigs of fresh coriander, to garnish
freshly cooked Thai rice and mixed
  shredded leek, celery, and red chilli,
  to serve

1 Place the celery, onion and leek in a large saucepan with the black peppercorns. Pour in 2 litres/3½ pints of hot water, bring to the boil and boil for 5 minutes, then immerse the lobster and boil for a further 8 minutes.

2 Remove the lobster. When cool enough to handle, sit it on its front. Using a sharp knife, halve the lobster neatly along its entire length. Remove and discard the intestinal vein from the tail, the stomach, (which lies near the head) and the inedible gills or dead man's fingers. Remove the meat from the shell and claws and cut into pieces.

3 Heat a wok or large frying pan, add the butter and when melted, add the raw prawns and fish stock. Stir-fry for 3 minutes or until the prawns change colour. Add the ginger, shallots, mushrooms, green peppercorns and oyster sauce. Season to taste with black pepper. Stir in the lobster. Stir-fry for 2–3 minutes.

4 Blend the cornflour with 1 teaspoon of water to form a thick paste, stir into the wok and cook, stirring, until the sauce thickens. Place the lobster on a warmed serving platter and tip the sauce over. Garnish and serve immediately.

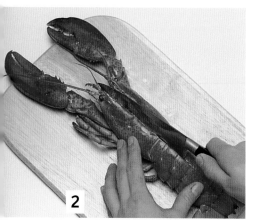

2

3

3

Louisiana Prawns & Fettuccine

INGREDIENTS

Serves 4

4 tbsp olive oil

450 g/1 lb raw tiger prawns, washed
   and peeled, shells and
   heads reserved

2 shallots, peeled and finely chopped

4 garlic cloves, peeled and
   finely chopped

large handful fresh basil leaves

1 carrot, peeled and finely chopped

1 onion, peeled and finely chopped

1 celery stick, trimmed and
   finely chopped

2–3 sprigs fresh parsley

2–3 sprigs fresh thyme

salt and freshly ground black pepper

pinch cayenne pepper

175 ml/6 fl oz dry white wine

450 g/1 lb ripe tomatoes,
   roughly chopped

juice of ½ lemon, or to taste

350 g/12 oz fettuccine

1 Heat 2 tablespoons of the olive oil in a large saucepan and add the reserved prawn shells and heads. Fry over a high heat for 2–3 minutes, until the shells turn pink and are lightly browned. Add half the shallots, half the garlic, half the basil and the carrot, onion, celery, parsley and thyme. Season lightly with salt, pepper and cayenne and sauté for 2–3 minutes, stirring often.

2 Pour in the wine and stir, scraping the pan well. Bring to the boil and simmer for 1 minute, then add the tomatoes. Cook for a further 3–4 minutes then pour in 200 ml/7 fl oz water. Bring to the boil, lower the heat and simmer for about 30 minutes, stirring often and using a wooden spoon to mash the prawn shells in order to release as much flavour as possible into the sauce. Lower the heat if the sauce is reducing very quickly.

3 Strain through a sieve, pressing well to extract as much liquid as possible; there should be about 450 ml/³/₄ pint. Pour the liquid into a clean pan and bring to the boil, then lower the heat and simmer gently until the liquid is reduced by about half.

4 Heat the remaining olive oil over a high heat in a clean frying pan and add the peeled prawns. Season lightly and add the lemon juice. Cook for 1 minute, lower the heat and add the remaining shallots and garlic. Cook for 1 minute. Add the sauce and adjust the seasoning.

5 Meanwhile, bring a large pan of lightly salted water to a rolling boil and add the fettuccine. Cook according to the packet instructions, or until 'al dente', and drain thoroughly. Transfer to a warmed serving dish. Add the sauce and toss well. Garnish with the remaining basil and serve immediately.

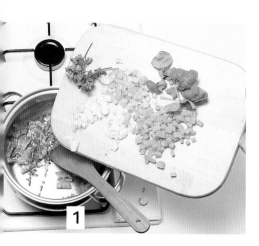

1

2

3

Stuffed Squid with Romesco Sauce

INGREDIENTS

Serves 4

8 small squid, about 350 g/12 oz
5 tbsp olive oil
50 g/2 oz pancetta, diced
1 onion, peeled and chopped
3 garlic cloves, peeled and
   finely chopped
2 tsp freshly chopped thyme
50 g/2 oz sun-dried tomatoes in oil
   drained, and chopped
75 g/3 oz fresh white breadcrumbs
2 tbsp freshly chopped basil
juice of ½ lime
salt and freshly ground black pepper
2 vine-ripened tomatoes, peeled and
   finely chopped
pinch of dried chilli flakes
1 tsp dried oregano
1 large red pepper, skinned
   and chopped
assorted salad leaves, to serve

1. Preheat oven to 230°C/450°F/Gas Mark 8, 15 minutes before cooking. Clean the squid if necessary, rinse lightly, pat dry with absorbent kitchen paper and finely chop the tentacles.

2. Heat 2 tablespoons of the olive oil in a large non-stick frying pan and fry the pancetta for 5 minutes, or until crisp. Remove the pancetta and reserve. Add the tentacles, onion, 2 garlic cloves, thyme and sun-dried tomatoes to the oil remaining in the pan and cook gently for 5 minutes, or until softened.

3. Remove the pan from the heat and stir in the diced pancetta. Blend in a food processor if a smoother stuffing is preferred, then stir in the breadcrumbs, basil and lime juice. Season to taste with salt and pepper and reserve. Spoon the stuffing into the cavity of the squid and secure the tops with cocktail sticks.

4. Place the squid in a large roasting tin, and sprinkle over 2 tablespoons each of oil and water. Place in the preheated oven and cook for 20 minutes.

5. Heat the remaining oil in a saucepan and cook the remaining garlic for 3 minutes. Add the tomatoes, chilli flakes and oregano and simmer gently for 15 minutes before stirring in the red pepper. Cook gently for a further 5 minutes. Blend in a food processor to make a smooth sauce and season to taste. Pour the sauce over the squid and serve immediately with some assorted salad leaves.

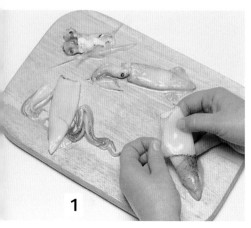

1

2

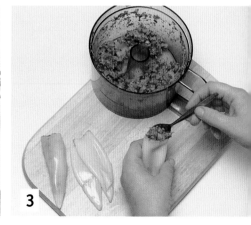

3

Scallops & Monkfish Kebabs with Fennel Sauce

INGREDIENTS

Serves 4

700 g/1½ lb monkfish tail
8 large fresh scallops
2 tbsp olive oil
1 garlic clove, peeled and crushed
freshly ground black pepper
1 fennel bulb, trimmed and
  thinly sliced
assorted salad leaves, to serve

For the sauce:

2 tbsp fennel seeds
pinch of chilli flakes
4 tbsp olive oil
2 tsp lemon juice
salt and freshly ground black pepper

1 Place the monkfish on a chopping board and remove the skin and the bone that runs down the centre of the tail and discard. Lightly rinse and pat dry with absorbent kitchen paper. Cut the two fillets into 12 equal-sized pieces and place in a shallow bowl.

2 Remove the scallops from their shells, if necessary, and clean thoroughly discarding the black vein. Rinse lightly and pat dry with absorbent kitchen paper. Put in the bowl with the fish.

3 Blend the 2 tablespoons of olive oil, the crushed garlic and a pinch of black pepper in a small bowl, then pour the mixture over the monkfish and scallops, making sure they are well coated. Cover lightly and leave to marinate in the refrigerator for at least 30 minutes, or longer if time permits. Spoon over the marinade occasionally.

4 Lightly crush the fennel seeds and chilli flakes in a pestle and mortar. Stir in the 4 tablespoons of olive oil and lemon juice and season to taste with salt and pepper. Cover and leave to infuse for 20 minutes.

5 Drain the monkfish and scallops, reserving the marinade and thread on to four skewers.

6 Spray a griddle pan with a fine spray of oil, then heat until almost smoking and cook the kebabs for 5–6 minutes, turning halfway through and brushing with the marinade throughout.

7 Brush the fennel slices with the fennel sauce and cook on the griddle for 1 minute on each side. Serve the fennel slices, topped with the kebabs and drizzled with the fennel sauce. Serve with a few assorted salad leaves.

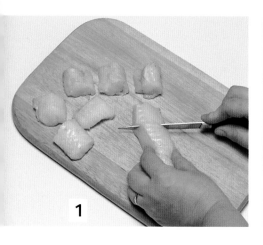
1

3

4

Red Pesto & Clam Spaghetti

INGREDIENTS

Serves 4

For the red pesto:

2 garlic cloves, peeled and
  finely chopped
50 g/2 oz pine nuts
25 g/1 oz fresh basil leaves
4 sun-dried tomatoes in oil, drained
4 tbsp olive oil
4 tbsp Parmesan cheese, grated
salt and freshly ground black pepper

For the clam sauce:

450 g/1 lb live clams, in their shells
1 tbsp olive oil
2 garlic cloves, peeled and crushed
1 small onion, peeled and chopped
5 tbsp medium dry white wine
150 ml/¼ pint fish or chicken stock
275 g/10 oz spaghetti

TASTY TIP

This dish looks particularly attractive with the clams left in their shells. If you prefer, you could remove the meat from the shells at the end of step 3, leaving just a few in for garnishing and stir back into the saucepan with the pasta.

1. To make the red pesto, place the garlic, pine nuts, basil leaves, sun-dried tomatoes and olive oil in a food processor and blend in short, sharp bursts until smooth. Scrape into a bowl, then stir in the Parmesan cheese and season to taste with salt and pepper. Cover and leave in the refrigerator until required.

2. Scrub the clams with a soft brush and remove any beards from the shells, discard any shells that are open or damaged. Wash in plenty of cold water then leave in a bowl covered with cold water in the refrigerator until required. Change the water frequently.

3. Heat the olive oil in a large saucepan and gently fry the garlic and onion for 5 minutes until softened, but not coloured. Add the wine and stock and bring to the boil. Add the clams, cover and cook for 3–4 minutes, or until the clams have opened.

4. Discard any clams that have not opened and stir in the red pesto sauce. Bring a large saucepan of lightly salted water to the boil and cook the spaghetti for 5–7 minutes, or until 'al dente'. Drain and return to the saucepan. Add the sauce to the spaghetti, mix well, then spoon into a serving dish and serve immediately.

Sardines in Vine Leaves

INGREDIENTS

Serves 4

8–16 vine leaves in brine, drained
2 spring onions
6 tbsp olive oil
2 tbsp lime juice
2 tbsp freshly chopped oregano
1 tsp mustard powder
salt and freshly ground black pepper
8 sardines, cleaned
8 bay leaves
8 sprigs of fresh dill

To garnish:
lime wedges
sprigs of fresh dill

To serve:
olive salad
crusty bread

1. Preheat the grill and line the grill rack with tinfoil just before cooking. Cut 8 pieces of string about 25.5 cm/10 inches long, and leave to soak in cold water for about 10 minutes. Cover the vine leaves in almost boiling water. Leave for 20 minutes, then drain and rinse thoroughly. Pat the vine leaves dry with absorbent kitchen paper.

2. Trim the spring onions and finely chop, then place into a small bowl. With a balloon whisk beat in the olive oil, lime juice, oregano, mustard powder and season to taste with salt and pepper. Cover with clingfilm and leave in the refrigerator, until required. Stir the mixture before using.

3. Prepare the sardines, by making two slashes on both sides of each fish and brush with a little of the lime juice mixture. Place a bay leaf and a dill sprig inside each sardine cavity and wrap with 1–2 vine leaves, depending on size. Brush with the lime mixture and tie the vine leaves in place with string.

4. Grill the fish for 4–5 minutes on each side under a medium heat, brushing with a little more of the lime mixture if necessary. Leave the fish to rest, unwrap and discard the vine leaves. Garnish with lime wedges and sprigs of fresh dill and serve with the remaining lime mixture, olive salad and crusty bread.

1

3

3

Parmesan & Garlic Lobster

INGREDIENTS

Serves 2

1 large cooked lobster
25 g/1 oz unsalted butter
4 garlic cloves, peeled and crushed
1 tbsp plain flour
300 ml/½ pint milk
125 g/4 oz Parmesan cheese, grated
sea salt and freshly ground
  black pepper
assorted salad leaves, to serve

FOOD FACT

Nowadays we consider lobster to be a luxury, however, up until the end of 19th century lobster was so plentiful that it was used as fish bait.

HELPFUL HINT

This impressive-looking dish makes a wonderful starter for two. Make the sauce in advance and cover the surface with a layer of clingfilm. Refrigerate until ready to use.

1 Preheat oven to 180°C/350°F/Gas Mark 4, 10 minutes before cooking. Halve the lobster and crack the claws. Remove the gills, the green sac behind the head and the black vein running down the body. Place the two lobster halves in a shallow ovenproof dish.

2 Melt the butter in a small saucepan and gently cook the garlic for 3 minutes, until softened. Add the flour and stir over a medium heat for 1 minute. Draw the saucepan off the heat then gradually stir in the milk, stirring until the sauce thickens. Return to the heat and cook for 2 minutes, stirring throughout until smooth and thickened. Stir in half the cheese and continue to cook for 1 minute, then season to taste with salt and pepper.

3 Pour the cheese sauce over the lobster halves and sprinkle with the remaining Parmesan cheese. Bake in the preheated oven for 20 minutes, or until heated through and the cheese sauce is golden brown. Serve with assorted salad leaves.

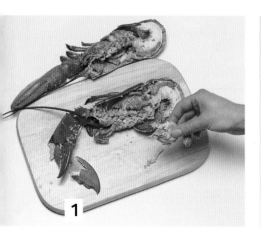
1

2

3

Roasted Monkfish with Parma Ham

INGREDIENTS

Serves 4

700 g/1½ lb monkfish tail
sea salt and freshly ground
   black pepper
4 bay leaves
4 slices fontina cheese, rind removed
8 slices Parma ham
225 g/8 oz angel hair pasta
50 g/2 oz butter
the zest and juice of 1 lemon
sprigs of fresh coriander, to garnish

To serve:
chargrilled courgettes
chargrilled tomatoes

HELPFUL HINT

Monkfish is also sold in boneless fillets, sometimes called loins. Remove the skin from the fish before cooking and if cubes or strips are required, remove the central bone.

1 Preheat oven to 200°C/400°F/Gas Mark 6, 15 minutes before cooking. Discard any skin from the monkfish tail and cut away and discard the central bone. Cut the fish into four equal-sized pieces and season to taste with salt and pepper and lay a bay leaf on each fillet, along with a slice of cheese.

2 Wrap each fillet with two slices of the Parma ham, so that the fish is covered completely. Tuck the ends of the Parma ham in and secure with a cocktail stick.

3 Lightly oil a baking sheet and place in the preheated oven for a few minutes. Place the fish on the preheated baking sheet, then place in the oven and cook for 12–15 minutes.

4 Bring a large saucepan of lightly salted water to the boil, then slowly add the pasta and cook for 5 minutes until 'al dente', or according to packet directions. Drain, reserving 2 tablespoons of the pasta-cooking liquor. Return the pasta to the saucepan and add the reserved pasta liquor, butter, lemon zest and juice. Toss until the pasta is well coated and glistening.

5 Twirl the pasta into small nests on four warmed serving plates and top with the monkfish parcels. Garnish with sprigs of coriander and serve with chargrilled courgettes and tomatoes.

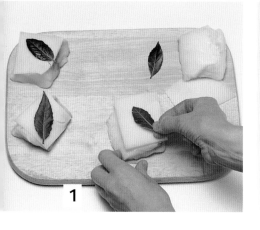
1

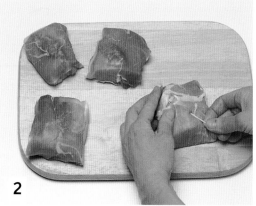
2

5

Mussels Arrabbiata

INGREDIENTS

Serves 4

1.8 kg/4 lb mussels
3–4 tbsp olive oil
1 large onion, peeled and sliced
4 garlic cloves, peeled and
   finely chopped
1 red chilli, deseeded and
   finely chopped
3 x 400 g cans chopped tomatoes
150 ml/¼ pint white wine
175 g/6 oz black olives, pitted
   and halved
salt and freshly ground black pepper
2 tbsp freshly chopped parsley
warm crusty bread, to serve

1   Clean the mussels by scrubbing with a small, soft brush, removing the beard and any barnacles from the shells. Discard any mussels that are open or have damaged shells. Place in a large bowl and cover with cold water. Change the water frequently before cooking and leave in the refrigerator until required.

2   Heat the olive oil in a large saucepan and sweat the onion, garlic and chilli until soft, but not coloured. Add the tomatoes and bring to the boil, then simmer for 15 minutes.

3   Add the white wine to the tomato sauce, bring the sauce to the boil and add the mussels. Cover and carefully shake the pan. Cook the mussels for 5–7 minutes, or until the shells have opened.

4   Add the olives to the pan and cook uncovered for about 5 minutes to warm through. Season to taste with salt and pepper and sprinkle in the chopped parsley. Discard any mussels that have not opened and serve immediately with lots of warm crusty bread.

FOOD FACT

Arrabbiata sauce is a classic Italian tomato-based sauce, usually containing onions, peppers, garlic and fresh herbs. It needs slow simmering to bring out the flavour and is excellent with meat, poultry and pasta as well as seafood.

Seared Tuna with Italian Salsa

INGREDIENTS

Serves 4

4 x 175 g/6 oz tuna or swordfish steaks
salt and freshly ground black pepper
3 tbsp Pernod
2 tbsp olive oil
zest and juice of 1 lemon
2 tsp fresh thyme leaves
2 tsp fennel seeds, lightly roasted
4 sun-dried tomatoes, chopped
1 tsp dried chilli flakes
assorted salad leaves, to serve

For the salsa:

1 white onion, peeled and
   finely chopped
2 tomatoes, deseeded and sliced
2 tbsp freshly shredded basil leaves
1 red chilli, deseeded and finely sliced
3 tbsp extra virgin olive oil
2 tsp balsamic vinegar
1 tsp caster sugar

1 Wipe the fish and season lightly with salt and pepper, then place in a shallow dish. Mix together the Pernod, olive oil, lemon zest and juice, thyme, fennel seeds, sun-dried tomatoes and chilli flakes and pour over the fish. Cover lightly and leave to marinate in a cool place for 1–2 hours, occasionally spooning the marinade over the fish.

2 Meanwhile, mix all the ingredients for the salsa together in a small bowl. Season to taste with salt and pepper, then cover and leave for about 30 minutes to allow all the flavours to develop.

3 Lightly oil a griddle pan and heat until hot. When the pan is very hot, drain the fish, reserving the marinade. Cook the fish for 3–4 minutes on each side, taking care not to overcook them – the tuna steaks should be a little pink inside. Pour any remaining marinade into a small saucepan, bring to the boil and boil for 1 minute. Serve the steaks hot with the marinade, chilled salsa and a few assorted salad leaves.

1

2

3

Pan–fried Salmon with Herb Risotto

INGREDIENTS

Serves 4

4 x 175 g/6 oz salmon fillets
3–4 tbsp plain flour
1 tsp dried mustard powder
salt and freshly ground black pepper
2 tbsp olive oil
3 shallots, peeled and chopped
225 g/8 oz Arborio rice
150 ml/¼ pint dry white wine
1.4 litres/2½ pints vegetable
  or fish stock
50 g/2 oz butter
2 tbsp freshly snipped chives
2 tbsp freshly chopped dill
2 tbsp freshly chopped flat-leaf parsley
knob of butter

To garnish:
slices of lemon
sprigs of fresh dill
tomato salad, to serve

1 Wipe the salmon fillets with a clean, damp cloth. Mix together the flour, mustard powder and seasoning on a large plate and use to coat the salmon fillets and reserve.

2 Heat half the olive oil in a large frying pan and fry the shallots for 5 minutes until softened, but not coloured. Add the rice and stir for 1 minute, then slowly add the wine, bring to the boil and boil rapidly until reduced by half.

3 Bring the stock to a gentle simmer, then add to the rice, a ladleful at a time. Cook, stirring frequently, until all the stock has been added and the rice is cooked but still retains a bite. Stir in the butter and freshly chopped herbs and season to taste with salt and pepper.

4 Heat the remaining olive oil and the knob of butter in a large griddle pan, add the salmon fillets and cook for 2–3 minutes on each side, or until cooked. Arrange the herb risotto on warm serving plates and top with the salmon. Garnish with slices of lemon and sprigs of dill and serve immediately with a tomato salad.

Sea Bass in Creamy Watercress & Prosciutto Sauce

INGREDIENTS

Serves 4

75 g/3 oz watercress
450 ml/³/₄ pint fish or chicken stock
150 ml/¹/₄ pint dry white wine
225 g/8 oz tagliatelle pasta
40 g/1¹/₂ oz butter
75 g/3 oz prosciutto ham
2 tbsp plain flour
300 ml/¹/₂ pint single cream
salt and freshly ground black pepper
olive oil, for spraying
4 x 175 g/6 oz sea bass fillets
fresh watercress, to garnish

1   Remove the leaves from the watercress stalks and reserve. Chop the stalks roughly and put in a large pan with the stock. Bring to the boil slowly, cover, and simmer for 20 minutes. Strain, and discard the stalks. Make the stock up to 300 ml/¹/₂ pint with the wine.

2   Bring a large saucepan of lightly salted water to the boil and cook the pasta for 8–10 minutes or until 'al dente'. Drain and reserve.

3   Melt the butter in a saucepan, and cook the prosciutto gently for 3 minutes. Remove with a slotted spoon. Stir the flour into the saucepan and cook on a medium heat for 2 minutes. Remove from the heat and gradually pour in the hot watercress stock, stirring continuously. Return to the heat and bring to the boil, stirring throughout. Simmer for 3 minutes, or until the sauce has thickened and is smooth. Purée the watercress leaves and cream in a food processor then add to the sauce with the prosciutto. Season to taste with salt and pepper, add the pasta, toss lightly and keep warm.

4   Meanwhile, spray a griddle pan lightly with olive oil, then heat until hot. When hot, cook the fillets for 3–4 minutes on each side, or until cooked. Arrange the sea bass on a bed of pasta and drizzle with a little sauce. Garnish with watercress and serve immediately.

HELPFUL HINT

Always wash watercress thoroughly before using, then either dry in a clean tea towel or a salad spinner to remove all the excess moisture.

1

3

3

Seafood Special

INGREDIENTS

Serves 4

2 tbsp olive oil

4 garlic cloves, peeled

125 g/4 oz squid, cut into rings

300 ml/½ pint medium-dry white wine

400 g can chopped tomatoes

2 tbsp fresh parsley, finely chopped

225 g/8 oz live mussels, cleaned and beards removed

125 g/4 oz monkfish fillet

125 g/4 oz fresh tuna

4 slices of Italian bread

To garnish:

225 g/8 oz large, unpeeled prawns, cooked

4 langoustines, cooked

3 tbsp freshly chopped parsley

TASTY TIP

This dish requires a well-flavoured bread – use a good-quality ciabatta or Pugliese loaf from an Italian delicatessen.

1. Heat the olive oil in a saucepan. Chop half of the garlic, add to the saucepan and gently cook for 1–2 minutes. Add the squid, 150 ml/¼ pint of the wine together with the tomatoes and simmer for 10–15 minutes.

2. Chop the remaining garlic and place with the remaining wine and 2 tablespoons of the parsley in another saucepan. Add the cleaned mussels to the pan, cover and cook for 7–8 minutes. Discard any mussels that have not opened, then remove the remaining mussels with a slotted spoon and add to the squid and tomato mixture. Reserve the liquor.

3. Cut the monkfish and tuna into chunks and place in the saucepan with the mussels' cooking liquor. Simmer for about 5 minutes, or until the fish is just tender.

4. Mix all the cooked fish and shellfish, with the exception of the prawns and langoustines, with the tomato mixture and cooking liquor in a large saucepan. Heat everything through until piping hot.

5. Toast the slices of bread and place in the base of a large, shallow serving dish.

6. Pour the fish mixture over the toasted bread and garnish with the prawns, langoustines and chopped parsley. Serve immediately.

1

3

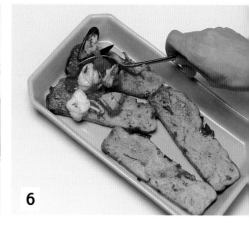

6

Farfalle with Smoked Trout in a Dill & Vodka Sauce

INGREDIENTS

Serves 4

400 g/14 oz farfalle
150 g/5 oz smoked trout
2 tsp lemon juice
200 ml/7 fl oz double cream
2 tsp wholegrain mustard
2 tbsp freshly chopped dill
4 tbsp vodka
salt and freshly ground black pepper
sprigs of dill, to garnish

FOOD FACT

Two types of smoked trout are available. One resembles smoked salmon in colour, texture and flavour, and can be cut into thin slivers as shown here. Equally delicious is hot smoked rainbow trout, which is available as a whole fish or in fillets. These should be skinned and the bones should be removed before use. The flesh can then be broken into large flakes. Smoked trout is fairly salty, so the sauce requires a minimal amount of seasoning with salt.

1 Bring a large pan of lightly salted water to a rolling boil. Add the pasta and cook according to the packet instructions, or until 'al dente'.

2 Meanwhile, cut the smoked trout into thin slivers, using scissors. Sprinkle lightly with the lemon juice and reserve.

3 Place the cream, mustard, chopped dill and vodka in a small pan. Season lightly with salt and pepper. Bring the contents of the pan to the boil and simmer gently for 2–3 minutes, or until slightly thickened.

4 Drain the cooked pasta thoroughly, then return to the pan. Add the smoked trout to the dill and vodka sauce, then pour over the pasta. Toss gently until the pasta is coated and the trout evenly mixed.

5 Spoon into a warmed serving dish or on to individual plates. Garnish with sprigs of dill and serve immediately.

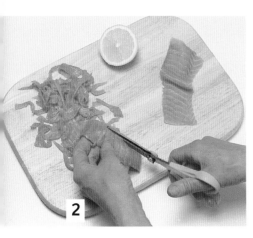

Pappardelle with Smoked Haddock & Blue Cheese Sauce

INGREDIENTS

Serves 4

350 g/12 oz smoked haddock

2 bay leaves

300 ml/½ pint milk

400 g/14 oz pappardelle or tagliatelle

25 g/1 oz butter

25 g/1 oz plain flour

150 ml/¼ pint single cream or
  extra milk

125 g/4 oz Dolcelatte cheese or
  Gorgonzola, cut into small pieces

¼ tsp freshly grated nutmeg

salt and freshly ground black pepper

40 g/1½ oz toasted walnuts, chopped

1 tbsp freshly chopped parsley

TASTY TIP

Dolcelatte is an Italian, semi-soft, blue-veined cheese made from cows' milk. It has a smooth creamy texture and a delicate taste. For a more strongly flavoured blue cheese sauce, a young Gorgonzola, Roquefort or blue Stilton can be used instead.

1 Place the smoked haddock in a saucepan with 1 bay leaf and pour in the milk. Bring to the boil slowly, cover and simmer for 6–7 minutes, or until the fish is opaque. Remove and roughly flake the fish, discarding the skin and any bones. Strain the milk and reserve.

2 Bring a large pan of lightly salted water to a rolling boil. Add the pasta and cook according to the packet instructions, or until 'al dente'.

3 Meanwhile, place the butter, flour and single cream or milk if preferred, in a pan and stir to mix. Stir in the reserved warm milk and add the remaining bay leaf. Bring to the boil, whisking all the time until smooth and thick. Gently simmer for 3–4 minutes, stirring frequently. Discard the bay leaf.

4 Add the Dolcelatte or Gorgonzola cheese to the sauce. Heat gently, stirring until melted. Add the flaked haddock and season to taste with nutmeg and salt and pepper.

5 Drain the pasta thoroughly and return to the pan. Add the sauce and toss gently to coat, taking care not to break up the flakes of fish. Tip into a warmed serving bowl, sprinkle with toasted walnuts and parsley and serve immediately.

1

3

4

Tuna & Macaroni Timbales

INGREDIENTS

Serves 4

125 g/4 oz macaroni
200 g can tuna in brine, drained
150 ml/¼ pint single cream
150 ml/¼ pint double cream
50 g/2 oz Gruyère cheese, grated
3 medium eggs, lightly beaten
salt and freshly ground black pepper
fresh chives, to garnish

For the fresh tomato dressing:

1 tsp Dijon mustard
1 tsp red wine vinegar
2 tbsp sunflower oil
1 tbsp hazelnut or walnut oil
350 g/12 oz firm ripe tomatoes,
    skinned, deseeded and chopped
2 tbsp freshly snipped chives

TASTY TIP

Other fish can be used to make these pasta timbales. Try a 200 g can of white crab meat, rinsed and drained, or pink salmon with all the bones removed.

1 Preheat the oven to 180°C/350°F/Gas Mark 4, 10 minutes before cooking. Oil and line the bases of four individual 150 ml/¼ pint timbales or ovenproof cups with non-stick baking parchment and stand in a small roasting tin.

2 Bring a large pan of lightly salted water to a rolling boil. Add the macaroni and cook according to the packet instructions, or until 'al dente'. Drain the cooked pasta thoroughly.

3 Flake the tuna fish and mix with the macaroni. Divide between the timbales or cups.

4 Pour the single and double cream into a small saucepan. Bring to the boil slowly, remove from the heat and stir in the Gruyère cheese until melted. Allow to cool for 1–2 minutes, then whisk into the beaten egg and season lightly with salt and pepper. Pour the mixture over the tuna fish and macaroni and cover each timbale with a small piece of tinfoil.

5 Pour enough hot water into the roasting tin to come halfway up the timbales. Place in the preheated oven and cook for 25 minutes. Remove the timbales from the water and allow to stand for 5 minutes.

6 For the tomato dressing, whisk together the mustard and vinegar in a small bowl, using a fork. Gradually whisk in the sunflower and nut oils, then stir in the chopped tomatoes and the snipped chives.

7 Unmould the timbales on to warmed serving plates and spoon the tomato dressing over the top and around the bottom. Garnish with fresh chives and serve immediately.

3

4

6

Seared Salmon & Lemon Linguine

INGREDIENTS

Serves 4

4 small skinless salmon fillets,
   each about 75 g/3 oz
2 tsp sunflower oil
1/2 tsp mixed or
   black peppercorns, crushed
400 g/14 oz linguine
15 g/1/2 oz unsalted butter
1 bunch spring onions, trimmed
   and shredded
300 ml/1/2 pint soured cream
zest of 1 lemon, finely grated
50 g/2 oz freshly grated
   Parmesan cheese
1 tbsp lemon juice
pinch of salt

To garnish:
dill sprigs
lemon slices

1 Brush the salmon fillets with the sunflower oil, sprinkle with crushed peppercorns and press on firmly and reserve.

2 Bring a large pan of lightly salted water to a rolling boil. Add the linguine and cook according to the packet instructions, or until 'al dente'.

3 Meanwhile, melt the butter in a saucepan and cook the shredded spring onions gently for 2–3 minutes, or until soft. Stir in the soured cream and the lemon zest and remove from the heat.

4 Preheat a griddle or heavy-based frying pan until very hot. Add the salmon and sear for 1 1/2–2 minutes on each side. Remove from the pan and allow to cool slightly.

5 Bring the soured cream sauce to the boil and stir in the Parmesan cheese and lemon juice. Drain the pasta thoroughly and return to the pan. Pour over the sauce and toss gently to coat.

6 Spoon the pasta on to warmed serving plates and top with the salmon fillets. Serve immediately with sprigs of dill and lemon slices.

1

3

4

Pan-fried Scallops & Pasta

INGREDIENTS

Serves 4

16 large scallops, shelled
1 tbsp olive oil
1 garlic clove, peeled and crushed
1 tsp freshly chopped thyme
400 g/14 oz penne
4 sun-dried tomatoes in oil, drained
  and thinly sliced
thyme or oregano sprigs, to garnish

For the tomato dressing:

2 sun-dried tomatoes in oil, drained
  and chopped
1 tbsp red wine vinegar
2 tsp balsamic vinegar
1 tsp sun-dried tomato paste
1 tsp caster sugar
salt and freshly ground black pepper
2 tbsp oil from a jar of
  sun-dried tomatoes
2 tbsp olive oil

1   Rinse the scallops and pat dry on absorbent kitchen paper. Place in a bowl and add the olive oil, crushed garlic and thyme. Cover and chill in the refrigerator until ready to cook.

2   Bring a large pan of lightly salted water to a rolling boil. Add the penne and cook according to the packet instructions, or until 'al dente'.

3   Meanwhile, make the dressing. Place the sun-dried tomatoes into a small bowl or glass jar and add the vinegars, tomato paste, sugar, salt and pepper. Whisk well, then pour into a food processor.

4   With the motor running, pour in the sun-dried tomato oil and olive oil in a steady stream to make a thick, smooth dressing.

5   Preheat a large, dry cast-iron griddle pan over a high heat for about 5 minutes. Lower the heat to medium then add the scallops to the pan. Cook for $1\frac{1}{2}$ minutes on each side. Remove from the pan.

6   Drain the pasta thoroughly and return to the pan. Add the sliced sun-dried tomatoes and dressing and toss. Divide between individual serving plates, top each portion with four scallops, garnish with fresh thyme or oregano sprigs and serve immediately.

1

3

5

Seafood Parcels with Pappardelle & Coriander Pesto

INGREDIENTS

Serves 4

300 g/11 oz pappardelle or tagliatelle
8 raw tiger prawns, shelled
12 raw queen scallops
225 g/8oz baby squid, cleaned and
  cut into rings
4 tbsp dry white wine
4 thin slices of lemon

Coriander pesto:

50 g/2 oz fresh coriander leaves
1 garlic clove, peeled
25 g/1 oz pine nuts, toasted
1 tsp lemon juice
5 tbsp olive oil
1 tbsp grated Parmesan cheese
salt and freshly ground black pepper

HELPFUL HINT

Prepare whole squid by firmly pulling the pouch and tentacles apart. Remove the transparent quill from the pouch and discard. Rinse the pouch under cold running water, then peel off the dark skin and discard.

1. Preheat the oven to 180°C/350°F/Gas Mark 4, 10 minutes before cooking. To make the pesto, blend the coriander leaves, garlic, pine nuts and lemon juice with 1 tablespoon of the olive oil to a smooth paste in a food processor. With the motor running slowly add the remaining oil. Stir the Parmesan cheese into the pesto and season to taste with salt and pepper.

2. Bring a pan of lightly salted water to a rolling boil. Add the pasta and cook for 3 minutes only. Drain thoroughly, return to the pan and spoon over two-thirds of the pesto. Toss to coat.

3. Cut out four circles, about 30 cm/12 in in diameter, from non-stick baking parchment. Spoon the pasta on to one half of each circle. Top each pile of pasta with two prawns, three scallops and a few squid rings. Spoon 1 tablespoon of wine over each serving, then drizzle with the remaining coriander pesto and top with a slice of lemon.

4. Close the parcels by folding over the other half of the paper, to make a semi-circle, then turn and twist the edges of the paper to secure.

5. Place the parcels on a baking tray and bake in the preheated oven for 15 minutes, or until cooked. Serve the parcels immediately, allowing each person to open their own.

1

3

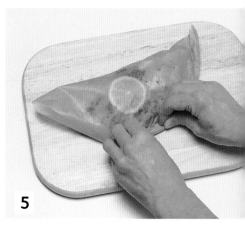

5

Spaghetti with Smoked Salmon & Tiger Prawns

INGREDIENTS

Serves 4

225 g/8 oz baby spinach leaves

salt and freshly ground black pepper

pinch freshly grated nutmeg

225 g/8 oz cooked tiger prawns in
  their shells, cooked

450 g/1 lb fresh angel hair spaghetti

50 g/2 oz butter

3 medium eggs

1 tbsp freshly chopped dill,
  plus extra to garnish

125 g/4 oz smoked salmon,
  cut into strips

dill sprigs, to garnish

2 tbsp grated Parmesan cheese,
  to serve

HELPFUL HINT

Make sure that you use cooked and not raw king prawns for this dish. If you buy them raw, remove the heads and shells then briefly sauté in a little olive oil until just pink and opaque. This will take only 3–4 minutes; take care not to overcook them or they will toughen.

1 Cook the baby spinach leaves in a large pan with 1 teaspoon of water for 3–4 minutes, or until wilted. Drain thoroughly, season to taste with salt, pepper and nutmeg and keep warm. Remove the shells from all but four of the tiger prawns and reserve.

2 Bring a large pan of lightly salted water to a rolling boil. Add the pasta and cook according to the packet instructions, about 3–4 minutes, or until 'al dente'. Drain thoroughly and return to the pan. Stir in the butter and the peeled prawns, cover and keep warm.

3 Beat the eggs with the dill, season well, then stir into the spaghettini and prawns. Return the pan to the heat briefly, just long enough to lightly scramble the eggs, then remove from the heat. Carefully mix in the smoked salmon strips and the cooked spinach. Toss gently to mix. Tip into a warmed serving dish and garnish with the reserved prawns and dill sprigs. Serve immediately with grated Parmesan cheese.

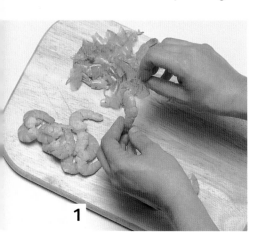

1

2

3

Conchiglioni with Crab au Gratin

INGREDIENTS

Serves 4

175 g/6 oz large pasta shells
50 g/2 oz butter
1 shallot, peeled and finely chopped
1 bird's eye chilli, deseeded and
  finely chopped
2 x 200 g cans crabmeat, drained
3 tbsp plain flour
50 ml/2 fl oz white wine
50 ml/2 fl oz milk
3 tbsp crème fraîche
15 g/½ oz Cheddar cheese, grated
salt and freshly ground black pepper
1 tbsp oil or melted butter
50 g/2 oz fresh white breadcrumbs

To serve:

cheese or tomato sauce
tossed green salad or freshly cooked
  baby vegetables

1 Preheat the oven to 200°C/400°F/Gas Mark 6, 15 minutes before cooking. Bring a large pan of lightly salted water to a rolling boil. Add the pasta shells and cook according to the packet instructions, or until 'al dente'. Drain thoroughly and allow to dry completely.

2 Melt half the butter in a heavy-based pan, add the shallots and chilli and cook for 2 minutes, then stir in the crabmeat. Stuff the cooled shells with the crab mixture and reserve.

3 Melt the remaining butter in a small pan and stir in the flour. Cook for 1 minute, then whisk in the wine and milk and cook, stirring, until thickened. Stir in the crème fraîche and grated cheese and season the sauce to taste with salt and pepper.

4 Place the crab filled shells in a lightly oiled, large shallow baking dish or tray and spoon a little of the sauce over. Toss the breadcrumbs in the melted butter or oil, then sprinkle over the pasta shells. Bake in the preheated oven for 10 minutes. Serve immediately with a cheese or tomato sauce and a tossed green salad or cooked baby vegetables.

2

1

4

Beef Fajitas with Avocado Sauce

INGREDIENTS

Serves 3–6

2 tbsp sunflower oil

450 g/1 lb beef fillet or rump steak, trimmed and cut into thin strips

2 garlic cloves, peeled and crushed

1 tsp ground cumin

¼ tsp cayenne pepper

1 tbsp paprika

230 g can chopped tomatoes

215 g can red kidney beans, drained

1 tbsp freshly chopped coriander

1 avocado, peeled, pitted and chopped

1 shallot, peeled and chopped

1 large tomato, skinned, deseeded and chopped

1 red chilli, diced

1 tbsp lemon juice

6 large flour tortilla pancakes

3–4 tbsp soured cream

green salad, to serve

1 Heat the wok, add the oil, then stir-fry the beef for 3–4 minutes. Add the garlic and spices and continue to cook for a further 2 minutes. Stir the tomatoes into the wok, bring to the boil, cover and simmer gently for 5 minutes.

2 Meanwhile, blend the kidney beans in a food processor until slightly broken up, then add to the wok. Continue to cook for a further 5 minutes, adding 2–3 tablespoons of water. The mixture should be thick and fairly dry. Stir in the chopped coriander.

3 Mix the chopped avocado, shallot, tomato, chilli and lemon juice together. Spoon into a serving dish and reserve.

4 When ready to serve, warm the tortillas and spread with a little soured cream. Place a spoonful of the beef mixture on top, followed by a spoonful of the avocado sauce, then roll up. Repeat until all the mixture is used up. Serve immediately with a green salad.

1

2

4

Pan-fried Beef with Creamy Mushrooms

INGREDIENTS

Serves 4

225 g/8 oz shallots, peeled
2 garlic cloves, peeled
2 tbsp olive oil
4 medallions of beef
4 plum tomatoes
125 g/4 oz flat mushrooms
3 tbsp brandy
150 ml/¼ pint red wine
salt and freshly ground black pepper
4 tbsp double cream

To serve:
baby new potatoes
freshly cooked green beans

1 Cut the shallots in half if large, then chop the garlic. Heat the oil in a large frying pan and cook the shallots for about 8 minutes, stirring occasionally, until almost softened. Add the garlic and beef and cook for 8–10 minutes, turning once during cooking until the meat is browned all over. Using a slotted spoon, transfer the beef to a plate and keep warm.

2 Rinse the tomatoes and cut into eighths, then wipe the mushrooms and slice. Add to the pan and cook for 5 minutes, stirring frequently until the mushrooms have softened.

3 Pour in the brandy and heat through. Draw the pan off the heat and carefully ignite. Allow the flames to subside. Pour in the wine, return to the heat and bring to the boil. Boil until reduced by one-third. Draw the pan off the heat, season to taste with salt and pepper, add the cream and stir.

4 Arrange the beef on serving plates and spoon over the sauce. Serve with baby new potatoes and a few green beans.

HELPFUL HINT

To prepare medallions of beef, buy a piece of fillet weighing approximately 700 g/1½ lb. Cut crosswise into four pieces.

Grilled Steaks with Saffron Potatoes & Roast Tomatoes

INGREDIENTS

Serves 4

700 g/1½ lb new potatoes, halved

few strands of saffron

300 ml/½ pint vegetable or beef stock

1 small onion, peeled and
   finely chopped

75 g/3 oz butter

salt and freshly ground black pepper

2 tsp balsamic vinegar

2 tbsp olive oil

1 tsp caster sugar

8 plum tomatoes, halved

4 boneless sirloin steaks, each
   weighing 225 g/8 oz

2 tbsp freshly chopped parsley

1 Cook the potatoes in boiling salted water for 8 minutes and drain well. Return the potatoes to the saucepan along with the saffron, stock, onion and 25 g/1 oz of the butter. Season to taste with salt and pepper and simmer, uncovered for 10 minutes until the potatoes are tender.

2 Meanwhile, preheat the grill to medium. Mix together the vinegar, olive oil, sugar and seasoning. Arrange the tomatoes cut-side up in a foil-lined grill pan and drizzle over the dressing. Grill for 12–15 minutes, basting occasionally, until tender.

3 Melt the remaining butter in a frying pan. Add the steaks and cook for 4–8 minutes to taste and depending on thickness.

4 Arrange the potatoes and tomatoes in the centre of four serving plates. Top with the steaks along with any pan juices. Sprinkle over the parsley and serve immediately.

Veal Escalopes with Marsala Sauce

INGREDIENTS

Serves 6

6 veal escalopes, about
  125 g/4 oz each
lemon juice
salt and freshly ground black pepper
6 sage leaves
6 slices prosciutto
2 tbsp olive oil
25 g/1 oz butter
1 onion, peeled and sliced
1 garlic clove, peeled and chopped
2 tbsp Marsala wine
4 tbsp double cream
2 tbsp freshly chopped parsley
sage leaves to garnish
selection of freshly cooked
  vegetables, to serve

TASTY TIP

If you prefer not to use veal, substitute with thinly sliced boneless pork loin or thin slices of turkey or chicken breast. You can substitute the sage leaves with basil sprigs and for a change add a little sliced cheese, such as Gruyère.

1 Place the veal escalopes between sheets of non-pvc clingfilm and using a mallet or rolling pin, pound lightly to flatten out thinly to about 5 mm/¼ inch thickness. Remove the clingfilm and sprinkle the veal escalopes with lemon juice, salt and black pepper.

2 Place a sage leaf in the centre of each escalope. Top with a slice of prosciutto making sure it just fits, then roll up the escalopes enclosing the prosciutto and sage leaves. Secure each escalope with a cocktail stick.

3 Heat the olive oil and butter in a large non-stick frying pan and fry the onions for 5 minutes, or until softened. Add the garlic and rolled escalopes and cook for about 8 minutes, turning occasionally, until the escalopes are browned all over.

4 Add the Marsala wine and cream to the pan and bring to the boil, cover and simmer for 10 minutes, or until the veal is tender. Season to taste and then sprinkle with the parsley. Discard the cocktail sticks and serve immediately with a selection of freshly cooked vegetables.

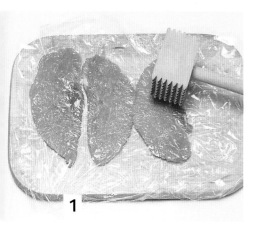

2

3

1

Fettuccine with Calves' Liver & Calvados

INGREDIENTS

Serves 4

450 g/1 lb calves' liver, trimmed
  and thinly sliced
50 g/2 oz plain flour
salt and freshly ground black pepper
1 tsp paprika
50 g/2 oz butter
1½ tbsp olive oil
2 tbsp Calvados
150 ml/¼ pint cider
150 ml/¼ pint whipping cream
350 g/12 oz fresh fettuccine
fresh thyme sprigs, to garnish

HELPFUL HINT

Calvados is made from apples and adds a fruity taste to this dish, although you can, of course, use ordinary brandy instead. Calves' liver is very tender, with a delicate flavour. It should be cooked over a high heat until the outside is brown and crusty and the centre still slightly pink. Take care not to overcook the liver or you will spoil its taste and texture.

1 Season the flour with the salt, black pepper and paprika, then toss the liver in the flour until well coated.

2 Melt half the butter and 1 tablespoon of the olive oil in a large frying pan and fry the liver in batches for 1 minute, or until just browned but still slightly pink inside. Remove using a slotted spoon and place in a warmed dish.

3 Add the remaining butter to the pan, stir in 1 tablespoon of the seasoned flour and cook for 1 minute. Pour in the Calvados and cider and cook over a high heat for 30 seconds. Stir the cream into the sauce and simmer for 1 minute to thicken slightly, then season to taste. Return the liver to the pan and heat through.

4 Bring a large pan of lightly salted water to a rolling boil. Add the fettuccine and cook according to the packet instructions, about 3–4 minutes, or until 'al dente'.

5 Drain the fettuccine thoroughly, return to the pan and toss in the remaining olive oil. Divide among four warmed plates and spoon the liver and sauce over the pasta. Garnish with thyme sprigs and serve immediately.

1

3

3

Tagliatelle with Stuffed Pork Escalopes

INGREDIENTS

Serves 4

150 g/5 oz broccoli florets, finely
  chopped and blanched
125 g/4 oz mozzarella cheese, grated
1 garlic clove, peeled and crushed
2 large eggs, beaten
salt and freshly ground black pepper
4 thin pork escalopes, weighing
  about 100 g/3½ oz each
1 tbsp olive oil
25 g/1 oz butter
2 tbsp flour
150 ml/¼ pint milk
150 ml/¼ pint chicken stock
1 tbsp Dijon mustard
225 g/8 oz fresh tagliatelle
sage leaves, to garnish

HELPFUL HINT

Pounding the pork escalopes
makes them thinner, but
tenderises the meat. Brush with a
little oil to prevent them sticking to
the mallet or rolling pin, or pound
(with the blunt side of the mallet)
between two sheets of oiled
greaseproof paper or clingfilm.
Take care not to tear the fibres.

1. Preheat the oven to 180°C/350°F/Gas Mark 4, 10 minutes before cooking. Mix the broccoli with the mozzarella cheese, garlic and beaten eggs. Season to taste with salt and pepper and reserve.

2. Using a meat mallet or rolling pin, pound the escalopes on a sheet of greaseproof paper until 5 mm/¼ inch thick. Divide the broccoli mixture between the escalopes and roll each one up from the shortest side. Place the pork rolls in a lightly oiled ovenproof dish, drizzle over the olive oil and bake in the preheated oven for 40–50 minutes, or until cooked.

3. Meanwhile, melt the butter in a heavy-based pan, stir in the flour and cook for 2 minutes. Remove from the heat and whisk in the milk and stock. Season to taste, stir in the mustard then cook until smooth and thickened. Keep warm.

4. Bring a large pan of lightly salted water to a rolling boil. Add the taglietelle and cook according to the packet instructions, about 3–4 minutes, or until 'al dente'. Drain thoroughly and tip into a warmed serving dish. Slice each pork roll into three, place on top of the pasta and pour the sauce over. Garnish with sage leaves and serve immediately.

1

2

3

Fettuccine with Wild Mushrooms & Prosciutto

INGREDIENTS

Serves 6

15 g/½ oz dried porcini mushrooms
150 ml/¼ pint hot chicken stock
2 tbsp olive oil
1 small onion, peeled and
　finely chopped
2 garlic cloves, peeled and
　finely chopped
4 slices prosciutto, chopped or torn
225 g/8 oz mixed wild or cultivated
　mushrooms, wiped and sliced
　if necessary
450 g/1 lb fettuccine
3 tbsp crème fraîche
2 tbsp freshly chopped parsley
salt and freshly ground black pepper
freshly grated Parmesan cheese,
　to serve (optional)

1　Place the dried mushrooms in a small bowl and pour over the hot chicken stock. Leave to soak for 15–20 minutes, or until the mushrooms have softened.

2　Meanwhile, heat the olive oil in a large frying pan. Add the onion and cook for 5 minutes over a medium heat, or until softened. Add the garlic and cook for 1 minute, then add the prosciutto and cook for a further minute.

3　Drain the dried mushrooms, reserving the soaking liquid. Roughly chop and add to the frying pan together with the fresh mushrooms. Cook over a high heat for 5 minutes, stirring often, or until softened. Strain the mushroom soaking liquid into the pan.

4　Meanwhile, bring a large pan of lightly salted water to a rolling boil. Add the pasta and cook according to the packet instructions, or until 'al dente'.

5　Stir the crème fraîche and chopped parsley into the mushroom mixture and heat through gently. Season to taste with salt and pepper. Drain the pasta well, transfer to a large warmed serving dish and pour over the sauce. Serve immediately with grated Parmesan cheese.

1

2

3

Crown Roast of Lamb

INGREDIENTS

Serves 6

1 lamb crown roast

salt and freshly ground black pepper

1 tbsp sunflower oil

1 small onion, peeled and
  finely chopped

2–3 garlic cloves, peeled and crushed

2 celery stalks, trimmed and
  finely chopped

125 g/4 oz cooked mixed basmati
  and wild rice

75 g/3 oz ready-to-eat-dried
  apricots, chopped

50 g/2 oz pine nuts, toasted

1 tbsp finely grated orange rind

2 tbsp freshly chopped coriander

1 small egg, beaten

freshly roasted potatoes and green
  vegetables, to serve

1   Preheat the oven to 180°C/350°F/Gas Mark 4, about 10 minutes before roasting. Wipe the crown roast and season the cavity with salt and pepper. Place in a roasting tin and cover the ends of the bones with small pieces of tinfoil.

2   Heat the oil in a small saucepan and cook the onion, garlic and celery for 5 minutes, then remove the saucepan from the heat. Add the cooked rice with the apricots, pine nuts, orange rind and coriander. Season with salt and pepper, then stir in the egg and mix well.

3   Carefully spoon the prepared stuffing into the cavity of the lamb, then roast in the preheated oven for 1–1½ hours. Remove the lamb from the oven and remove and discard the tinfoil from the bones. Return to the oven and continue to cook for a further 15 minutes, or until cooked to personal preference.

4   Remove from the oven and leave to rest for 10 minutes before serving with the roast potatoes and freshly cooked vegetables.

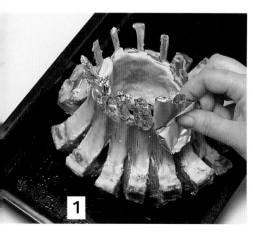

1

2

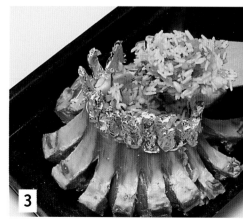

3

Spicy Chicken Skewers with Mango Tabbouleh

INGREDIENTS

Serves 4

400 g/14 oz chicken breast fillet

200 ml/7 fl oz natural low-fat yogurt

1 garlic clove, peeled and crushed

1 small red chilli, deseeded and
finely chopped

½ tsp ground turmeric

finely grated rind and juice
of ½ lemon

sprigs of fresh mint, to garnish

For the mango tabbouleh:

175 g/6 oz bulgur wheat

1 tsp olive oil

juice of ½ lemon

½ red onion, finely chopped

1 ripe mango, halved, stoned,
peeled and chopped

¼ cucumber, finely diced

2 tbsp freshly chopped parsley

2 tbsp freshly shredded mint

salt and finely ground
black pepper

1 If using wooden skewers, pre-soak them in cold water for at least 30 minutes. (This stops them from burning during grilling.)

2 Cut the chicken into 5 x 1 cm/2 x ½ inch strips and place in a shallow dish.

3 Mix together the yogurt, garlic, chilli, turmeric, lemon rind and juice. Pour over the chicken and toss to coat. Cover and leave to marinate in the refrigerator for up to 8 hours.

4 To make the tabbouleh, put the bulgur wheat in a bowl. Pour over enough boiling water to cover. Put a plate over the bowl. Leave to soak for 20 minutes.

5 Whisk together the oil and lemon juice in a bowl. Add the red onion and leave to marinade for 10 minutes.

6 Drain the bulgur wheat and squeeze out any excess moisture in a clean tea towel. Add to the red onion with the mango, cucumber, herbs and season to taste with salt and pepper. Toss together.

7 Thread the chicken strips on to eight wooden or metal skewers. Cook under a hot grill for 8 minutes. Turn and brush with the marinade, until the chicken is lightly browned and cooked through.

8 Spoon the tabbouleh on to individual plates. Arrange the chicken skewers on top and garnish with the sprigs of mint. Serve warm or cold.

3

4

6

Chicken with Porcini Mushrooms & Cream

INGREDIENTS

Serves 4

2 tbsp olive oil

4 boneless chicken breasts,
    preferably free range

2 garlic cloves, peeled and crushed

150 ml/¼ pint dry vermouth or
    dry white wine

salt and freshly ground black pepper

25 g/1 oz butter

450 g/1 lb porcini or wild
    mushrooms, thickly sliced

1 tbsp freshly chopped oregano

sprigs of fresh basil,
    to garnish (optional)

freshly cooked rice, to serve

TASTY TIP

Porcini or cep mushrooms grow wild and are relatively easy to find, if you know where to look. They can, however, be very expensive to buy fresh. If they are unavailable, substitute with fresh button or chestnut mushrooms and 15 g/ ½ oz reconstituted dried porcini instead.

1 Heat the olive oil in a large, heavy-based frying pan, then add the chicken breasts, skin-side down and cook for about 10 minutes, or until they are well browned. Remove the chicken breasts and reserve. Add the garlic, stir into the juices and cook for 1 minute.

2 Pour the vermouth or white wine into the pan and season to taste with salt and pepper. Return the chicken to the pan. Bring to the boil, reduce the heat to low and simmer for about 20 minutes, or until tender.

3 In another large frying pan, heat the butter and add the sliced porcini or wild mushrooms. Stir-fry for about 5 minutes, or until the mushrooms are golden and tender.

4 Add the porcini or wild mushrooms and any juices to the chicken. Season to taste, then add the chopped oregano. Stir together gently and cook for 1 minute longer. Transfer to a large serving plate and garnish with sprigs of fresh basil, if desired. Serve immediately with rice.

2

3

4

Pasta Ring with Chicken & Sun-dried Tomatoes

INGREDIENTS

Serves 6

125 g/4 oz butter, plus extra
   for brushing
2 tbsp natural white breadcrumbs
40 g/1½ oz flour
450 ml/¾ pint milk
1 small onion, peeled and very
   finely chopped
salt and freshly ground black pepper
225 g/8 oz fresh tagliatelle
450 g/1 lb chicken breast fillets,
   skinned and cut into strips
200 ml/7 fl oz white wine
1 tsp cornflour
2 tbsp freshly chopped tarragon
2 tbsp chopped sun-dried tomatoes

HELPFUL HINT

To ensure that the pasta turns out easily, brush the ring mould with melted butter, then put in the freezer for 3–4 minutes to harden. Brush again with butter before dusting with the breadcrumbs, making sure it is well coated.

1. Preheat the oven to 190°C/375°F/Gas Mark 5, 10 minutes before cooking. Lightly brush a 20.5 cm/8 inch ring mould with a little melted butter and dust with the breadcrumbs.

2. Melt 50 g/2 oz of the butter in a heavy-based pan. Add the flour and cook for 1 minute. Whisk in the milk and cook, stirring, until thickened. Add the chopped onion, season to taste with salt and pepper and reserve.

3. Bring a large pan of lightly salted water to a rolling boil. Add the tagliatelle and cook according to the packet instructions, about 3–4 minutes, or until 'al dente'. Drain thoroughly and stir into the white sauce. Pour the pasta mixture into the prepared mould and bake in the preheated oven for 25–30 minutes.

4. Melt the remaining butter in a frying pan, add the chicken and cook for 4–5 minutes, or until cooked. Pour in the wine and cook over a high heat for 30 seconds. Blend the cornflour with 1 teaspoon of water and stir into the pan. Add 1 tablespoon chopped tarragon and the tomatoes. Season well, then cook for a few minutes, until thickened.

5. Allow the pasta to cool for 5 minutes, then unmould on to a large serving plate. Fill the centre with the chicken sauce. Garnish with the remaining tarragon and serve immediately.

1

3

4

Spicy Chicken with Open Ravioli & Tomato Sauce

INGREDIENTS

Serves 2–3

2 tbsp olive oil

1 onion, peeled and finely chopped

1 tsp ground cumin

1 tsp hot paprika pepper

1 tsp ground cinnamon

175 g/6 oz boneless and skinless chicken breasts, chopped

salt and freshly ground black pepper

1 tbsp smooth peanut butter

50 g/2 oz butter

1 shallot, peeled and finely chopped

2 garlic cloves, peeled and crushed

400 g can chopped tomatoes

125 g/4 oz fresh egg lasagne

2 tbsp freshly chopped coriander

HELPFUL HINT

Remember that fresh pasta should be exactly that; buy no more than two days ahead. Because it contains fresh eggs it should always be stored in the refrigerator, kept in its packet or wrapped in non-stick baking parchment, then in clingfilm.

1 Heat the olive oil in a frying pan, add the onion and cook gently for 2–3 minutes then add the cumin, paprika pepper and cinnamon and cook for a further 1 minute. Add the chicken, season to taste with salt and pepper and cook for 3–4 minutes, or until tender. Add the peanut butter and stir until well mixed and reserve.

2 Melt the butter in the frying pan, add the shallot and cook for 2 minutes. Add the tomatoes and garlic and season to taste. Simmer gently for 20 minutes, or until thickened, then keep the sauce warm.

3 Cut each sheet of lasagne into six squares. Bring a large pan of lightly salted water to a rolling boil. Add the lasagne squares and cook according to the packet instructions, about 3–4 minutes, or until 'al dente'. Drain the lasagne pieces thoroughly, reserve and keep warm.

4 Layer the pasta squares with the spicy filling on individual warmed plates. Pour over a little of the hot tomato sauce and sprinkle with chopped coriander. Serve immediately.

1

3

4

Chilli Roast Chicken

INGREDIENTS

Serves 4

3 medium-hot fresh
  red chillies, deseeded

½ tsp ground turmeric

1 tsp cumin seeds

1 tsp coriander seeds

2 garlic cloves, peeled and crushed

2.5 cm/1 inch piece fresh root ginger,
  peeled and chopped

1 tbsp lemon juice

1 tbsp olive oil

2 tbsp roughly chopped fresh coriander

½ tsp salt

freshly ground black pepper

1.4 kg/3 lb oven-ready chicken

15 g/½ oz unsalted butter, melted

550 g/1¼ lb butternut squash

fresh parsley and coriander sprigs,
  to garnish

To serve:

4 baked potatoes

seasonal green vegetables

1 Preheat the oven to 190°C/375°F/Gas Mark 5. Roughly chop the chillies and put in a food processor with the turmeric, cumin seeds, coriander seeds, garlic, ginger, lemon juice, olive oil, coriander, salt, pepper and 2 tablespoons of cold water. Blend to a paste, leaving the ingredients still slightly chunky.

2 Starting at the neck end of the chicken, gently ease up the skin to loosen it from the breast. Reserve 3 tablespoons of the paste. Push the remaining paste over the chicken breast under the skin, spreading it evenly.

3 Put the chicken in a large roasting tin. Mix the reserved chilli paste with the melted butter. Use 1 tablespoon to brush evenly over the chicken, roast in the preheated oven for 20 minutes.

4 Meanwhile, halve, peel and scoop out the seeds from the butternut squash. Cut into large chunks and mix in the remaining chilli paste and butter mixture.

5 Arrange the butternut squash around the chicken. Roast for a further hour, basting with the cooking juices about every 20 minutes until the chicken is fully cooked and the squash tender. Garnish with parsley and coriander. Serve hot with baked potatoes and green vegetables.

1

2

4

Chicken & Prawn–stacked Ravioli

INGREDIENTS

Serves 4

1 tbsp olive oil

1 onion, peeled and chopped

1 garlic clove, peeled and chopped

450 g/1 lb boned and skinned cooked
   chicken, cut into large pieces

1 beefsteak tomato, deseeded
   and chopped

150 ml/¼ pint dry white wine

150 ml/¼ pint double cream

250 g/9 oz peeled cooked prawns,
   thawed if frozen

2 tbsp freshly chopped tarragon,
   plus sprigs to garnish

salt and freshly ground black pepper

8 sheets fresh lasagne

HELPFUL HINT

Always check the packet instructions when cooking lasagne; some brands may need longer cooking than others. It should be cooked until 'al dente' – tender, but firm to the bite. Dried lasagne – either plain or verde – may be used instead of fresh if preferred, but it will take longer to cook.

1 Heat the olive oil in a large frying pan, add the onion and garlic and cook for 5 minutes, or until softened, stirring occasionally. Add the chicken pieces and fry for 4 minutes, or until heated through, turning occasionally.

2 Stir in the chopped tomato, wine and cream and bring to the boil. Lower the heat and simmer for about 5 minutes, or until reduced and thickened. Stir in the prawns and tarragon and season to taste with salt and pepper. Heat the sauce through gently.

3 Meanwhile, bring a large pan of lightly salted water to the boil and add two lasagne sheets. Return to the boil and cook for 2 minutes, stirring gently to avoid sticking. Remove from the pan using a slotted spoon and keep warm. Repeat with the remaining sheets.

4 Cut each sheet of lasagne in half. Place two pieces on each of the warmed plates and divide half of the chicken mixture among them. Top each serving with a second sheet of lasagne and divide the remainder of the chicken mixture among them. Top with a final layer of lasagne. Garnish with tarragon sprigs and serve immediately.

1

3

4

Grilled Spiced Chicken with Tomato & Shallot Chutney

INGREDIENTS

Serves 4

3 tbsp sunflower oil

2 hot red chillies, deseeded
  and chopped

3 garlic cloves, peeled and chopped

1 tsp ground turmeric

1 tsp cumin seeds

1 tsp fennel seeds

1 tbsp freshly chopped basil

1 tbsp dark brown sugar

125 ml/4 fl oz rice or white
  wine vinegar

2 tsp sesame oil

4 large chicken breast quarters,
  wings attached

225 g/8 oz small shallots, peeled
  and halved

2 tbsp Chinese rice wine or dry sherry

50 g/2 oz caster sugar

175 g/6 oz cherry tomatoes, halved

2 tbsp light soy sauce

To garnish:

sprigs of fresh coriander

sprigs of fresh dill

lemon wedges

1 Preheat the grill to medium, 5 minutes before cooking. Heat a wok or large frying pan, add 1 tablespoon of the sunflower oil and when hot, add the chillies, garlic, turmeric, cumin, fennel seeds, and basil. Fry for 5 minutes, add the sugar and 2 tablespoons of vinegar and stir until the sugar has dissolved. Remove, stir in the sesame oil and leave to cool.

2 Cut three or four deep slashes in the thickest part of the chicken breasts. Spread the spice paste over the chicken, place in a dish, cover and marinate in the refrigerator for at least 4 hours or overnight.

3 Heat the remaining sunflower oil in a saucepan, add the shallots and remaining garlic and cook gently for 15 minutes. Add the remaining vinegar, Chinese rice wine or sherry and caster sugar with 50 ml/2 fl oz water. Bring to the boil and simmer rapidly for 10 minutes, or until thickened. Add the tomatoes with the soy sauce. Simmer for 5–10 minutes, or until the liquid is reduced. Leave the chutney to cool.

4 Transfer the chicken pieces to a grill pan and cook under the preheated grill for 15–20 minutes on each side, or until the chicken is cooked through, basting frequently. Garnish with coriander sprigs and lemon wedges and serve immediately with the chutney.

Wild Rice & Bacon Salad with Smoked Chicken

INGREDIENTS

Serves 4

150 g/5 oz wild rice
50 g/2 oz pecan or walnut halves
1 tbsp vegetable oil
4 slices smoked bacon, diced
3–4 shallots, peeled and
  finely chopped
75 ml/3 fl oz walnut oil
2–3 tbsp sherry or cider vinegar
2 tbsp freshly chopped dill
salt and freshly ground black pepper
275 g/10 oz smoked chicken or duck
  breast, thinly sliced
dill sprigs, to garnish

FOOD FACT

Both smoked chicken and duck have a delicate smoky flavour which comes from being first cold-smoked, then briefly hot-smoked. You can, of course, use plain roasted chicken or duck if you prefer.

1 Put the wild rice in a medium saucepan with 600 ml/1 pint water and bring to the boil, stirring once or twice. Reduce the heat, cover and simmer gently for 30–50 minutes, depending on the texture you prefer, chewy or tender. Using a fork, gently fluff into a large bowl and leave to cool slightly.

2 Meanwhile, toast the nuts in a frying pan over a medium heat for 2 minutes, or until they are fragrant and lightly coloured, stirring and tossing frequently. Cool, then chop coarsely and add to the rice.

3 Heat the oil in the frying pan over a medium heat. Add the bacon and cook, stirring from time to time, for 3–4 minutes, or until crisp and brown. Remove from the pan and drain on absorbent kitchen paper. Add the shallots to the pan and cook for 4 minutes, or until just softened, stirring from time to time. Stir into the rice and nuts, with the drained bacon pieces.

4 Whisk the walnut oil, vinegar, half the dill and salt and pepper in a small bowl until combined. Pour the dressing over the rice mixture and toss well to combine. Mix the chicken and the remaining chopped dill into the rice, then spoon into bowls and garnish each serving with a dill sprig. Serve slightly warm, or at room temperature.

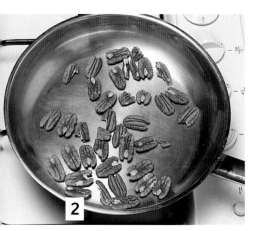

2

3

4

Turkey Escalopes Marsala with Wilted Watercress

INGREDIENTS

Serves 4

4 turkey escalopes, each about
  150 g/5 oz
25 g/1 oz plain flour
1/2 tsp dried thyme
salt and freshly ground black pepper
1–2 tbsp olive oil
125 g/4 oz watercress
40 g/1 1/2 oz butter
225 g/8 oz mushrooms, wiped
  and quartered
50 ml/2 fl oz dry Marsala wine
50 ml/2 fl oz chicken stock or water

HELPFUL HINT

Turkey escalopes are simply thin slices of turkey breast fillets which have been flattened. If they are unavailable, substitute chicken breasts that have been halved horizontally and flattened between pieces of clingfilm.

1 Place each turkey escalope between two sheets of non-stick baking parchment and using a meat mallet or rolling pin pound to make an escalope about 3 mm/⅛ inch thick. Put the flour in a shallow dish, add the thyme, season to taste with salt and pepper and stir to blend. Coat each escalope lightly on both sides with the flour mixture, then reserve.

2 Heat the olive oil in a large frying pan, then add the watercress and stir-fry for about 2 minutes, until just wilted and brightly coloured. Season with salt and pepper. Using a slotted spoon, transfer the watercress to a plate and keep warm.

3 Add half the butter to the frying pan and when melted, add the mushrooms. Stir-fry for 4 minutes, or until golden and tender. Remove from the pan and reserve.

4 Add the remaining butter to the pan and, working in batches if necessary, cook the flour-coated escalopes for 2–3 minutes on each side, or until golden and cooked thoroughly, adding the remaining oil, if necessary. Remove from the pan and keep warm.

5 Add the Marsala wine to the pan and stir, scraping up any browned bits from the bottom of the pan. Add the stock or water and bring to the boil over a high heat. Season lightly.

6 Return the escalopes and mushrooms to the pan and reheat gently until piping hot. Divide the warm watercress between four serving plates.

7 Arrange one escalope over each serving of wilted watercress and spoon over the mushrooms and Marsala sauce. Serve immediately.

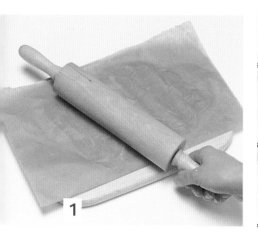
2

4

1

Chinese Barbecue–style Quails with Aubergines

INGREDIENTS

Serves 4

4 quails

2 tbsp salt

3 tbsp hoisin sauce

1 tbsp Chinese rice wine or dry sherry

1 tbsp light soy sauce

700 g/1½ lb aubergines, trimmed
  and cubed

1 tbsp oil

4 garlic cloves, peeled and
  finely chopped

1 tbsp freshly chopped root ginger

6 spring onions, trimmed and
  finely chopped

3 tbsp dark soy sauce

¼ tsp dried chilli flakes

1 tbsp yellow bean sauce

1 tbsp sugar

To garnish:

sprigs of fresh coriander

sliced red chilli

1 Preheat the oven to 240°C/475°F/Gas Mark 9. Rub the quails inside and out with 1 tablespoon of the salt. Mix together the hoisin sauce, Chinese rice wine or sherry and light soy sauce. Rub the quails inside and out with the sauce. Transfer to a small roasting tin and roast in the preheated oven for 5 minutes. Reduce the heat to 180°C/350°F/Gas Mark 4 and continue to roast for 20 minutes. Turn the oven off and leave the quails for 5 minutes, then remove and leave to rest for 10 minutes.

2 Place the aubergine in a colander and sprinkle with the remaining salt. Leave to drain for 20 minutes, then rinse under cold running water and pat dry with absorbent kitchen paper.

3 Heat a wok or large frying pan over a moderate heat. Add the oil and when hot, add the aubergines, garlic, ginger and four of the spring onions and cook for 1 minute. Add the dark soy sauce, chilli flakes, yellow bean sauce, sugar and 450 ml/¾ pint of water. Bring to the boil, then simmer uncovered for 10–15 minutes.

4 Increase the heat to high and continue to cook, stirring occasionally, until the sauce is reduced and slightly thickened. Spoon the aubergine mixture on to warmed individual plates and top with a quail. Garnish with the remaining spring onion, fresh chilli and a sprig of coriander and serve immediately.

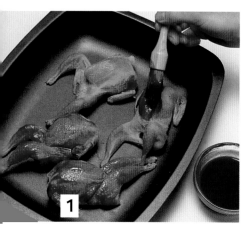

Pheasant with Portabella Mushrooms & Red Wine Gravy

INGREDIENTS

Serves 4

25 g/1 oz butter

1 tbsp olive oil

2 small pheasants (preferably hens) rinsed, well dried and halved

8 shallots, peeled

300 g/11 oz portabella mushrooms, thickly sliced

2–3 sprigs of fresh thyme or rosemary, leaves stripped

300 ml/½ pint Valpolicella or fruity red wine

300 ml/½ pint hot chicken stock

1 tbsp cornflour

2 tbsp balsamic vinegar

2 tbsp redcurrant jelly, or to taste

2 tbsp freshly chopped flat-leaf parsley

salt and freshly ground black pepper

sprigs of fresh thyme, to garnish

1 Preheat oven to 180°C/350°F/Gas Mark 4. Heat the butter and oil in a large saucepan or frying pan. Add the pheasant halves and shallots working in batches, if necessary, and cook for 10 minutes, or until golden on all sides, shaking the pan to glaze the shallots. Transfer to a casserole dish large enough to hold the pieces in a single layer. Add the mushroom and thyme to the pan and cook for 2–3 minutes, or until beginning to colour. Transfer to the dish with the pheasant halves.

2 Add the wine to the saucepan, it will bubble and steam. Cook, stirring up any browned bits from the pan and allow to reduce by half. Pour in the stock and bring to the boil, then pour over the pheasant halves. Cover and braise in the preheated oven for 50 minutes, or until tender. Remove the pheasant halves and vegetables to a wide, shallow serving dish and set the casserole or roasting tin over a medium-high heat.

3 Skim off any surface fat and bring to the boil. Blend the cornflour with the vinegar and stir into the sauce with the redcurrant jelly. Boil until the sauce is reduced and thickened slightly. Stir in the parsley and season to taste with salt and pepper. Pour over the pheasant halves, garnish with sprigs of fresh thyme and serve immediately.

1

1

3

Pheasant with Sage & Blueberries

INGREDIENTS

Serves 4

3 tbsp olive oil

3 shallots, peeled and
  coarsely chopped

2 sprigs of fresh sage,
  coarsely chopped

1 bay leaf

1 lemon, halved

salt and freshly ground black pepper

2 pheasants or guinea fowl, rinsed
  and dried

125 g/4 oz blueberries

4 slices Parma ham or bacon

125 ml/4 fl oz vermouth or
  dry white wine

200 ml/⅓ pint chicken stock

3 tbsp double cream or butter
  (optional)

1 tbsp brandy

roast potatoes, to serve

1 Preheat oven to 180°C/350°F/Gas Mark 4, 10 minutes before cooking. Place the oil, shallots, sage and bay leaf in a bowl, with the juice from the lemon halves. Season with salt and pepper. Tuck each of the squeezed lemon halves into the birds with 75 g/3 oz of the blueberries, then rub the birds with the marinade and leave for 2–3 hours, basting occasionally.

2 Remove the birds from the marinade and cover each with two slices of Parma ham. Tie the legs of each bird with string and place in a roasting tin. Pour over the marinade and add the vermouth. Roast in the preheated oven for 1 hour, or until tender and golden and the juices run clear when a thigh is pierced with a sharp knife or skewer.

3 Transfer to a warm serving plate, cover with tinfoil and discard the string. Skim off any surface fat from the tin and set over a medium-high heat.

4 Add the stock to the tin and bring to the boil, scraping any browned bits from the bottom. Boil until slightly reduced. Whisk in the cream or butter, if using, and simmer until thickened, whisking constantly. Stir in the brandy and strain into a gravy jug. Add the remaining blueberries and keep warm.

5 Using a sharp carving knife, cut each of the birds in half and arrange on the plate with the crispy Parma ham. Serve immediately with roast potatoes and the gravy.

1

2

5

Spatchcocked Poussins with Garlic Sage Butter

INGREDIENTS

Serves 4

For the herb butter:

6 large garlic cloves
150 g/5 oz butter, softened
2 tbsp freshly snipped chives
2 tbsp freshly chopped sage
grated rind and juice of 1 small lemon
salt and freshly ground black pepper

For the poussins:

4 spatchcocked poussins
2 tbsp extra virgin olive oil

To garnish:

chives
fresh sage leaves

To serve:

grilled polenta (see page 70)
grilled tomatoes

1 Preheat the grill or light an outdoor charcoal grill and line the grill rack with tinfoil, just before cooking. Put the garlic cloves in a small saucepan and cover with cold water. Bring to the boil, then simmer for 5 minutes, or until softened. Drain and cool slightly. Cut off the root end of each clove and squeeze the softened garlic into a bowl.

2 Pound the garlic until smooth, then beat in the butter, chives, sage and lemon rind and juice. Season to taste with salt and pepper.

3 Using your fingertips, gently loosen the skin from each poussin breast by sliding your hand between the skin and the flesh. Push one-quarter of the herb butter under the skin, spreading evenly over the breast and the top of the thighs. Pull the neck skin gently to tighten the skin over the breast and tuck under the bird. Repeat with the remaining birds and herb butter.

4 Thread two wooden skewers crossways through each bird, from one wing through the opposite leg, to keep the poussin flat. Repeat with the remaining birds, brush with the olive oil and season with salt and pepper.

5 Arrange the poussins on the rack over the foil-lined rack and grill for 25 minutes, turning occasionally, until golden and crisp and the juices run clear when a thigh is pierced with a sharp knife or skewer. Position the rack about 12.5 cm/5 inches from the heat source or the skin will brown before the birds are cooked through. Garnish with chives and sage leaves and serve immediately with grilled polenta and a few grilled tomatoes.

2

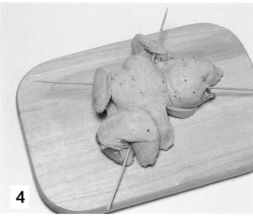
4

5

Crispy Roast Duck Legs with Pancakes

INGREDIENTS

Serves 6

900 g/2 lb plums, halved

25 g/1 oz butter

2 star anise

1 tsp freshly grated root ginger

50 g/2 oz soft brown sugar

zest and juice of 1 orange

salt and freshly ground black pepper

4 duck legs

3 tbsp dark soy sauce

2 tbsp dark brown sugar

½ cucumber, cut into matchsticks

1 small bunch spring onions,
  trimmed and shredded

18 ready-made Chinese
  pancakes, warmed

1 Preheat the oven to 220°C/425°F/Gas Mark 7, 15 minutes before cooking. Discard stones from plums and place in a saucepan with the butter, star anise, ginger, brown sugar and orange zest and juice. Season to taste with pepper. Cook over a gentle heat until the sugar has dissolved. Bring to the boil, then reduce heat and simmer for 15 minutes, stirring occasionally until the plums are soft and the mixture is thick. Remove the star anise. Leave to cool.

2 Using a fork, prick the duck legs all over. Place in a large bowl and pour boiling water over to remove some of the fat. Drain, pat dry on absorbent kitchen paper and leave until cold.

3 Mix together the soy sauce, dark brown sugar and the ½ teaspoon of salt. Rub this mixture generously over the duck legs. Transfer to a wire rack set over a roasting tin and roast in the preheated oven for 30–40 minutes, or until well cooked and the skin is browned and crisp. Remove from the oven and leave to rest for 10 minutes.

4 Shred the duck meat using a fork to hold the hot duck leg and another to remove the meat. Transfer to a warmed serving platter with the cucumber and spring onions. Serve immediately with the plum compote and warmed pancakes.

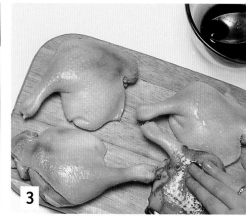

Aromatic Duck Burgers on Potato Pancakes

INGREDIENTS

Serves 4

700 g/1½ lb boneless duck breasts
2 tbsp hoisin sauce
1 garlic clove, peeled and finely
   chopped
4 spring onions, trimmed and finely
   chopped
2 tbsp Japanese soy sauce
½ tsp Chinese five spice powder
salt and freshly ground black pepper
freshly chopped coriander, to garnish
extra hoisin sauce, to serve

For the potato pancakes:
450 g/1 lb floury potatoes
1 small onion, peeled and grated
1 small egg, beaten
1 heaped tbsp plain flour

1   Peel off the thick layer of fat from the duck breasts and cut into small pieces. Put the fat in a small dry saucepan and set over a low heat for 10–15 minutes, or until the fat runs clear and the crackling goes crisp; reserve.

2   Cut the duck meat into pieces and blend in a food processor until coarsely chopped. Spoon into a bowl and add the hoisin sauce, garlic, half the spring onions, soy sauce and Chinese five spice powder. Season to taste with salt and pepper and shape into four burgers. Cover and chill in the refrigerator for 1 hour.

3   To make the potato pancakes, grate the potatoes into a large bowl, squeeze out the water with your hands, then put on a clean tea towel and twist the ends to squeeze out any remaining water. Return the potato to the bowl, add the onion and egg and mix well. Add the flour and salt and pepper. Stir to blend.

4   Heat about 2 tablespoons of the clear duck fat in a large frying pan. Spoon the potato mixture into 4–8 pattie shapes and cook for 6 minutes, or until golden and crisp, turning once. Keep warm in the oven. Repeat with the remaining mixture, adding duck fat as needed.

5   Preheat the grill and line the grill rack with tinfoil. Brush the burgers with a little of the duck fat and grill for 6–8 minutes, or longer if wished, turning once. Arrange 1–2 potato pancakes on a plate and top with a burger. Spoon over a little hoisin sauce and garnish with the remaining spring onions and coriander.

1

3

4

Duck Lasagne with Porcini & Basil

INGREDIENTS

Serves 6

1.4–1.8 kg/3–4 lb duck, quartered
1 onion, unpeeled and quartered
2 carrots, peeled and cut into pieces
1 celery stalk, cut into pieces
1 leek, trimmed and cut into pieces
2 garlic cloves, unpeeled
  and smashed
1 tbsp black peppercorns
2 bay leaves
6–8 sprigs of fresh thyme
50 g/2 oz dried porcini mushrooms
125 ml/4 oz dry sherry
75 g/3 oz butter, diced
1 bunch of fresh basil leaves,
  stripped from stems
24 pre-cooked lasagne sheets
75 g/3 oz Parmesan cheese, grated
sprig of parsley, to garnish
mixed salad, to serve

1 Preheat the oven to 180°C/350°F/Gas Mark 4, 10 minutes before cooking. Put the duck with the vegetables, garlic, peppercorns, bay leaves and thyme into a large stock pot and cover with cold water. Bring to the boil, skimming off any fat, then reduce the heat and simmer for 1 hour. Transfer the duck to a bowl and cool slightly.

2 When cool enough to handle, remove the meat from the duck and dice. Return all the bones and trimmings to the simmering stock and continue to simmer for 1 hour. Strain the stock into a large bowl and leave until cold. Remove and discard the fat that has risen to the top of the stock.

3 Put the porcini in a colander and rinse under cold running water. Leave for 1 minute to dry off, then turn out on to a chopping board and chop finely. Place in a small bowl, then pour over the sherry and leave for about 1 hour, or until the porcini are plump and all the sherry is absorbed.

4 Heat 25 g/1 oz of the butter in a frying pan. Shred the basil leaves and add to the hot butter, stirring until wilted. Add the soaked porcini and any liquid, mix well and reserve.

5 Oil a 30.5 x 23 cm/12 x 9 inch deep baking dish and pour a little stock into the base. Cover with six to eight lasagne sheets, making sure that sheets slightly overlap. Continue to layer the pasta with a little stock, duck meat, the mushroom-basil mixture and Parmesan. Add a little butter every other layer.

6 Cover with tinfoil and bake in the preheated oven for 40–45 minutes, or until cooked. Stand for 10 minutes before serving. Garnish with a sprig of parsley and serve with salad.

Honey–glazed Duck in Kumquat Sauce

INGREDIENTS

Serves 4

4 duck breast fillets
1 tbsp light soy sauce
1 tsp sesame oil
1 tbsp clear honey
3 tbsp brandy
1 tbsp sunflower oil
2 tbsp caster sugar
1 tbsp white wine vinegar
150 ml/¼ pint orange juice
125 g/4 oz kumquats, thinly sliced
2 tsp cornflour
salt and freshly ground black pepper
fresh watercress, to garnish
basmati and wild rice, to serve

1   Thinly slice the duck breasts and put in a shallow bowl. Mix together the soy sauce, sesame oil, honey and 1 tablespoon of brandy. Pour over the duck, stir well, cover and marinate in the refrigerator for at least 1 hour.

2   Heat a wok until hot, add the sunflower oil and swirl it round to coat the sides. Drain the duck, reserving the marinade, and stir-fry over a high heat for 2–3 minutes, or until browned. Remove from the wok; reserve.

3   Wipe the wok clean with absorbent kitchen paper. Add the sugar, vinegar and 1 tablespoon of water. Gently heat until the sugar dissolves, then boil until a rich golden colour. Pour in the orange juice, then the remaining brandy. Stir in the kumquat slices and simmer for 5 minutes.

4   Blend the cornflour with 1 tablespoon of cold water. Add to the wok and simmer for 2–3 minutes, stirring until thickened. Return the duck to the wok and cook gently for 1–2 minutes, or until warmed through. Season to taste with salt and pepper. Spoon onto warmed plates and garnish with fresh watercress leaves. Serve immediately with freshly cooked basmati and wild rice.

1

3

4

Spinach & Ricotta Gnocchi with Butter & Parmesan

INGREDIENTS

Serves 2–4

125 g/4 oz frozen leaf spinach, thawed
225 g/8 oz ricotta cheese
2 small eggs, lightly beaten
50 g/2 oz freshly grated
   Parmesan cheese
salt and freshly ground black pepper
2 tbsp freshly chopped basil
50 g/2 oz plain flour
50 g/2 oz unsalted butter
2 garlic cloves, peeled and crushed
Parmesan cheese shavings, to serve

FOOD FACT

Ricotta is a crumbly, soft white cheese made from ewes' milk whey, a by-product from the manufacture of Pecorino Romano cheese. The curd is compacted so that the cheese can be cut with a knife. It can be eaten by itself, but normally it is used in dishes such as cheesecake.

1 Squeeze the excess moisture from the spinach and chop finely. Blend in a food processor with the ricotta cheese, eggs, Parmesan cheese, seasoning and 1 tablespoon of the basil until smooth. Scrape into a bowl then add sufficient flour to form a soft, slightly sticky dough.

2 Bring a large pan of salted water to a rolling boil. Transfer the spinach mixture to a piping bag fitted with a large plain nozzle. As soon as the water is boiling, pipe 10–12 short lengths of the mixture into the water, using a sharp knife to cut the gnocchi as you go.

3 Bring the water back to the boil and cook the gnocchi for 3–4 minutes, or until they begin to rise to the surface. Remove with a slotted spoon, drain on absorbent kitchen paper and transfer to a warmed serving dish. Cook the gnocchi in batches if necessary.

4 Melt the butter in a small frying pan and when foaming add the garlic and remaining basil. Remove from the heat and immediately pour over the cooked gnocchi. Season well with salt and pepper and serve immediately with extra grated Parmesan cheese.

1

2

3

Aubergine Cannelloni with Watercress Sauce

INGREDIENTS

Serves 4

4 large aubergines, about
  250 g/9 oz each
5–6 tbsp olive oil
350 g/12 oz ricotta cheese
75 g/3 oz Parmesan cheese, grated
3 tbsp freshly chopped basil
salt and freshly ground black pepper

For the watercress sauce:

75 g/3 oz watercress, trimmed
200 ml/¹/₃ pint vegetable stock
1 shallot, peeled and sliced
pared strip of lemon rind
1 large sprig of thyme
3 tbsp crème fraîche
1 tsp lemon juice

To garnish:

sprigs of watercress
lemon zest

1 Preheat oven to 190°C/375°F/Gas Mark 5, 10 minutes before cooking. Cut the aubergines lengthways into thin slices, discarding the side pieces. Heat 2 tablespoons of oil in a frying pan and cook the aubergine slices in a single layer in several batches, turning once, until golden on both sides.

2 Mix the cheeses, basil and seasoning together. Lay the aubergine slices on a clean surface and spread the cheese mixture evenly between them.

3 Roll up the slices from one of the short ends to enclose the filling. Place, seam-side down in a single layer in an ovenproof dish. Bake in the preheated oven for 15 minutes, or until golden.

4 To make the watercress sauce, blanch the watercress leaves in boiling water for about 30 seconds. Drain well, then rinse in a sieve under cold running water and squeeze dry. Put the stock, shallot, lemon rind and thyme in a small saucepan. Boil rapidly until reduced by half, then remove from the heat and strain.

5 Put the watercress and strained stock in a food processor and blend until fairly smooth. Return to the saucepan, stir in the crème fraîche, lemon juice and season to taste with salt and pepper. Heat gently until the sauce is piping hot.

6 Serve a little of the sauce drizzled over the aubergines and the rest separately in a jug. Garnish the cannelloni with sprigs of watercress and lemon zest. Serve immediately.

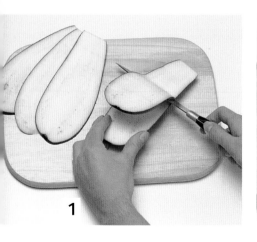
1

2

5

Pastini-stuffed Peppers

INGREDIENTS

Serves 6

6 red, yellow or orange peppers, tops
    cut off and deseeded
salt and freshly ground black pepper
175 g/6 oz pastini
4 tbsp olive oil
1 onion, peeled and finely chopped
2 garlic cloves, peeled and
    finely chopped
3 ripe plum tomatoes, skinned,
    deseeded and chopped
50 ml/2 fl oz dry white wine
8 pitted black olives, chopped
4 tbsp freshly chopped mixed herbs,
    such as parsley, basil, oregano
    or marjoram
125 g/4 oz mozzarella cheese, diced
4 tbsp grated Parmesan cheese
fresh tomato sauce, preferably
    home-made, to serve

1 Preheat the oven to 190°C/375°F/Gas Mark 5, 10 minutes before cooking. Bring a pan of water to the boil. Trim the bottom of each pepper so it sits straight. Blanch the peppers for 2–3 minutes, then drain on absorbent kitchen paper.

2 Return the water to the boil, add ½ teaspoon of salt and the pastini and cook for 3–4 minutes, or until 'al dente'. Drain thoroughly, reserving the water. Rinse under cold running water, drain again and reserve.

3 Heat 2 tablespoons of the olive oil in a large frying pan, add the onion and cook for 3–4 minutes. Add the garlic and cook for 1 minute. Stir in the tomatoes and wine and cook for 5 minutes, stirring frequently. Add the olives, herbs, mozzarella cheese and half the Parmesan cheese. Season to taste with salt and pepper. Remove from the heat and stir in the pastini.

4 Dry the insides of the peppers with absorbent kitchen paper, then season lightly. Arrange the peppers in a lightly oiled shallow baking dish and fill with the pastini mixture. Sprinkle with the remaining Parmesan cheese and drizzle over the remaining oil. Pour in boiling water to come 1 cm/½ inch up the sides of the dish. Cook in the preheated oven for 25 minutes, or until cooked. Serve immediately with freshly made tomato sauce.

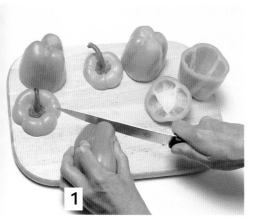

1

3

4

Penne with Vodka & Caviar

INGREDIENTS

Serves 4

400 g/14 oz penne

25 g/1 oz butter

4–6 spring onions, trimmed and
thinly sliced

1 garlic clove, peeled and finely
chopped

125 ml/4 fl oz vodka

200 ml/7 fl oz double cream

1–2 ripe plum tomatoes, skinned,
deseeded and chopped

75 g/3 oz caviar

salt and freshly ground black pepper

FOOD FACT

Authentic sturgeon caviar is very expensive. Red caviar from salmon, or black or red lump-fish roe, can be substituted. Alternatively, 175 g/6 oz thinly sliced smoked salmon pieces, can also be substituted. Sturgeon caviar has a salty flavour, so always check the taste before adding salt. Smoked salmon and lump-fish roe have a much saltier taste, however, so no additional salt would be necessary.

1 Bring a large pan of lightly salted water to a rolling boil. Add the penne and cook according to the packet instructions, or until 'al dente'. Drain thoroughly and reserve.

2 Heat the butter in a large frying pan or wok, add the spring onions and stir-fry for 1 minute. Stir in the garlic and cook for a further 1 minute. Pour the vodka into the pan; it will bubble and steam. Cook until the vodka is reduced by about half, then add the double cream and return to the boil. Simmer gently for 2–3 minutes, or until the sauce has thickened slightly.

3 Stir in the tomatoes, then stir in all but 1 tablespoon of the caviar and season to taste with salt and pepper. Add the penne and toss lightly to coat. Cook for 1 minute, or until heated through. Divide the mixture among four warmed pasta bowls and garnish with the reserved caviar. Serve immediately.

Gnocchi Roulade with Mozzarella & Spinach

INGREDIENTS

Serves 8

600 ml/1 pint milk
125 g/4 oz fine semolina or polenta
25 g/1 oz butter
75 g/3 oz Cheddar cheese, grated
2 medium egg yolks
salt and freshly ground black pepper
700 g/1½ lb baby spinach leaves
½ tsp freshly grated nutmeg
1 garlic clove, peeled and crushed
2 tbsp olive oil
150 g/5 oz mozzarella cheese, grated
2 tbsp freshly grated Parmesan cheese
freshly made tomato sauce, to serve

HELPFUL HINT

It is important to use the correct size of tin for this dish, so that the gnocchi mixture is thin enough to roll up. Do not be tempted to put it in the refrigerator to cool or it will become too hard and crack when rolled.

1   Preheat the oven to 240°C/475°F/Gas Mark 9, 15 minutes before cooking. Oil and line a large Swiss roll tin (23 x 33 cm/9 x 13 inch) with non-stick baking parchment.

2   Pour the milk into a heavy-based pan and whisk in the semolina. Bring to the boil then simmer, stirring continuously with a wooden spoon, for 3–4 minutes, or until very thick. Remove from heat and stir in the butter and Cheddar cheese until melted. Whisk in the egg yolks and season to taste with salt and pepper. Pour into the lined tin. Cover and allow to cool for 1 hour.

3   Cook the baby spinach in batches in a large pan with 1 teaspoon of water for 3–4 minutes, or until wilted. Drain thoroughly, season to taste with salt, pepper and nutmeg, then allow to cool.

4   Spread the spinach over the cooled semolina mixture and sprinkle over 75 g/3 oz of the mozzarella and half the Parmesan cheese. Bake in the preheated oven for 20 minutes, or until golden.

5   Allow to cool, then roll up like a Swiss roll. Sprinkle with the remaining mozzarella and Parmesan cheese, then bake for another 15–20 minutes, or until golden. Serve immediately with freshly made tomato sauce.

2

4

5

Cannelloni with Tomato & Red Wine Sauce

INGREDIENTS

Serves 6

2 tbsp olive oil

1 onion, peeled and finely chopped

1 garlic clove, peeled and crushed

250 g carton ricotta cheese

50 g/2 oz pine nuts

salt and freshly ground black pepper

pinch freshly grated nutmeg

250 g/9 oz fresh spinach lasagne

25 g/1 oz butter

1 shallot, peeled and finely chopped

150 ml/¼ pint red wine

400 g can chopped tomatoes

½ tsp sugar

50 g/2 oz mozzarella cheese, grated,
   plus extra to serve

1 tbsp freshly chopped parsley,
   to garnish

fresh green salad, to serve

1. Preheat the oven to 200°C/400°F/Gas Mark 6, 15 minutes before cooking. Heat the oil in a heavy-based pan, add the onion and garlic and cook for 2–3 minutes. Cool slightly, then stir in the ricotta cheese and pine nuts. Season the filling to taste with salt, pepper and the nutmeg.

2. Cut each lasagne sheet in half, put a little of the ricotta filling on each piece and roll up like a cigar to resemble cannelloni tubes. Arrange the cannelloni, seam-side down, in a single layer, in a lightly oiled, 2.3 litre/4 pint shallow ovenproof dish.

3. Melt the butter in a pan, add the shallot and cook for 2 minutes. Pour in the red wine, tomatoes and sugar and season well. Bring to the boil, lower the heat and simmer for about 20 minutes, or until thickened. Add a little more sugar if desired. Transfer to a food processor and blend until a smooth sauce is formed.

4. Pour the warm tomato sauce over the cannelloni and sprinkle with the grated mozzarella cheese. Bake in the preheated oven for about 30 minutes, or until golden and bubbling. Garnish and serve immediately with a green salad.

1

2

4

Individual Steamed Chocolate Puddings

INGREDIENTS

Serves 8

150 g/5 oz unsalted butter, softened

175 g/6 oz light muscovado sugar

½ tsp freshly grated nutmeg

25 g/1 oz plain white flour, sifted

4 tbsp cocoa powder, sifted

5 medium eggs, separated

125 g/4 oz ground almonds

50 g/2 oz fresh white breadcrumbs

To serve:

Greek yogurt

orange-flavoured chocolate curls

HELPFUL HINT

Look for individual plastic pudding basins for making this recipe. They are very easy to unmould, as you simply squeeze them to release the pudding.

1　Preheat the oven to 180°C/350°F/Gas Mark 4, 10 minutes before baking. Lightly oil and line the bases of eight individual 175 ml/6 fl oz pudding basins with a small circle of nonstick baking parchment. Cream the butter with 50 g/2 oz of the sugar and the nutmeg until light and fluffy.

2　Sift the flour and cocoa powder together, then stir into the creamed mixture. Beat in the egg yolks and mix well, then fold in the ground almonds and the breadcrumbs.

3　Whisk the egg whites in a clean grease-free bowl until stiff and standing in peaks then gradually whisk in the remaining sugar. Using a metal spoon, fold a quarter of the egg whites into the chocolate mixture and mix well, then fold in the remaining egg whites.

4　Spoon the mixture into the prepared basins, filling them two-thirds full to allow for expansion. Cover with a double sheet of tinfoil and secure tightly with string. Stand the pudding basins in a roasting tin and pour in sufficient water to come halfway up the sides of the basins.

5　Bake in the centre of the preheated oven for 30 minutes, or until the puddings are firm to the touch. Remove from the oven, loosen around the edges and invert onto warmed serving plates. Serve immediately with Greek yogurt and chocolate curls.

Crème Brûlée with Sugared Raspberries

INGREDIENTS

Serves 6

600 ml/1 pint fresh whipping cream

4 medium egg yolks

75 g/3 oz caster sugar

½ tsp vanilla essence

25 g/1 oz demerara sugar

175 g/6 oz fresh raspberries

HELPFUL HINT

Most chefs use blow torches to brown the sugar in step 5, as this is the quickest way to caramelise the top of the dessert. Take great care if using a blow torch, especially when lighting. Otherwise use the grill, making sure that it is very hot and the dessert is thoroughly chilled before caramelising the sugar topping. This will prevent the custard underneath from melting.

1 Preheat the oven to 150°C/300°F/Gas Mark 2. Pour the cream into a bowl and place over a saucepan of gently simmering water. Heat gently but do not allow to boil.

2 Meanwhile, whisk together the egg yolks, 50 g/2 oz of the caster sugar and the vanilla essence. When the cream is warm, pour it over the egg mixture briskly whisking until it is mixed completely.

3 Pour into six individual ramekin dishes and place in a roasting tin.

4 Fill the tin with sufficient water to come halfway up the sides of the dishes.

5 Bake in the preheated oven for about 1 hour, or until the puddings are set. (To test if set, carefully insert a round bladed knife into the centre, if the knife comes out clean they are set.)

6 Remove the puddings from the roasting tin and allow to cool. Chill in the refrigerator, preferably overnight.

7 Sprinkle the sugar over the top of each dish and place the puddings under a preheated hot grill.

8 When the sugar has caramelised and turned deep brown, remove from the heat and cool. Chill the puddings in the refrigerator for 2–3 hours before serving.

9 Toss the raspberries in the remaining caster sugar and sprinkle over the top of each dish. Serve with a little extra cream if liked.

2

5

7

Golden Castle Pudding

INGREDIENTS

Serves 4-6

125 g/4 oz butter
125 g/4 oz caster sugar
a few drops of vanilla essence
2 medium eggs, beaten
125 g/4 oz self-raising flour
4 tbsp golden syrup
crème fraîche or ready-made custard,
   to serve

1   Preheat the oven to 180°C/350°F/Gas Mark 4. Lightly oil four to six individual pudding bowls and place a small circle of lightly oiled non-stick baking or greaseproof paper in the base of each one.

2   Place the butter and caster sugar in a large bowl, then beat together until the mixture is pale and creamy. Stir in the vanilla essence and gradually add the beaten eggs, a little at a time. Add a tablespoon of flour after each addition of egg and beat well.

3   When the mixture is smooth, add the remaining flour and fold in gently. Add a tablespoon of water and mix to form a soft mixture that will drop easily off a spoon.

4   Spoon enough mixture into each basin to come halfway up, allowing enough space for the puddings to rise. Place on a baking sheet and bake in the preheated oven for about 25 minutes until firm and golden brown.

5   Allow the puddings to stand for 5 minutes. Discard the paper circle and turn out on to individual serving plates.

6   Warm the golden syrup in a small saucepan and pour a little over each pudding. Serve hot with the crème fraîche or custard.

HELPFUL HINT

For a change, make the traditional Castle Pudding by placing a spoonful of jam in the base of each basin. Top with the sponge and bake.

1

4

6

Raspberry Chocolate Ganache & Berry Tartlets

INGREDIENTS

Serves 8

For the chocolate pastry:

125 g/4 oz unsalted butter, softened

60 g/2½ oz caster sugar

2 tsp vanilla essence

175 g/6 oz plain flour, sifted

40 g/1½ oz cocoa powder

For the filling:

600 ml/1 pint whipping cream

275 g/10 oz seedless raspberry jam

225 g/8 oz plain dark
  chocolate, chopped

700 g/1½ lb raspberries or other
  summer berries

50 ml/2 fl oz framboise liqueur

1 tbsp caster sugar

crème fraîche, to serve

TASTY TIP

Try substituting an equal quantity of white chocolate for the plain chocolate in this recipe, as raspberries go very well with it.

1 Preheat the oven to 200°C/400°F/Gas Mark 6, 15 minutes before cooking. Make the chocolate pastry by putting the butter, sugar and vanilla essence into a food processor and blending until creamy. Add the flour and cocoa powder and process until a soft dough forms. Wrap in clingfilm, chill for at least 1 hour, and then use to line eight 7.5 cm/3 inch tartlet tins. Bake blind in the preheated oven for 12 minutes.

2 Place 400 ml/14 fl oz of the cream and half of the raspberry jam in a saucepan and bring to the boil, whisking constantly to dissolve the jam. Remove from the heat and add the chocolate all at once, stirring until the chocolate has melted.

3 Pour into the pastry-lined tartlet tins, shaking gently to distribute the ganache evenly. Chill in the refrigerator for 1 hour or until set.

4 Place the berries in a large shallow bowl. Heat the remaining raspberry jam with half the framboise liqueur over a medium heat until melted and bubbling. Drizzle over the berries and toss gently to coat.

5 Divide the berries among the tartlets, piling them up if necessary. Chill in the refrigerator until ready to serve.

6 Remove the tartlets from the refrigerator for at least 30 minutes before serving. Using an electric whisk, whisk the remaining cream with the caster sugar and the remaining framboise liqueur until it is thick and softly peaking. Serve with the tartlets and crème fraîche.

1

2

3

White Chocolate Mousse & Strawberry Tart

INGREDIENTS

Cuts into 10 slices

1 quantity shop-bought sweet shortcrust pastry
60 g/2½ oz strawberry jam
1–2 tbsp kirsch or framboise liqueur
450–700 g/1–1½ lb ripe strawberries, sliced lengthways

For the white chocolate mousse:

250 g/9 oz white chocolate, chopped
350 ml/12 oz double cream
3 tbsp kirsch or framboise liqueur
1–2 large egg whites (optional)

HELPFUL HINT

This recipe contains raw egg whites, which should be eaten with caution by vulnerable groups including the elderly, young and pregnant women. If you are worried, omit them from the recipe.

1 Preheat the oven to 200°C/400°F/Gas Mark 6, 15 minutes before baking. Roll the prepared pastry out on a lightly floured surface and use to line a 25.5 cm/10 inch flan tin.

2 Line with either tinfoil or nonstick baking parchment and baking beans then bake blind in the preheated oven for 15–20 minutes. Remove the tinfoil or baking parchment and return to the oven for a further 5 minutes.

3 To make the mousse, place the white chocolate with 2 tablespoons of water and 125 ml/4 fl oz of the cream in a saucepan and heat gently, stirring until the chocolate has melted and is smooth. Remove from the heat, stir in the kirsch or framboise liqueur and cool.

4 Whip the remaining cream until soft peaks form. Fold a spoonful of the cream into the cooled white chocolate mixture, then fold in the remaining cream. If using, whisk the egg whites until stiff and gently fold into the white chocolate cream mixture to make a softer, lighter mousse. Chill in the refrigerator for 15–20 minutes.

5 Heat the strawberry jam with the kirsch or framboise liqueur and brush or spread half the mixture onto the pastry base. Leave to cool.

6 Spread the chilled chocolate mousse over the jam and arrange the sliced strawberries in concentric circles over the mousse. If necessary, reheat the strawberry jam and glaze the strawberries lightly.

7 Chill the tart in the refrigerator for about 3–4 hours, or until the chocolate mousse has set. Cut into slices and serve.

3

4

6

Chocolate Profiteroles

INGREDIENTS

Serves 4

For the pastry:

150 ml/¼ pint water
50 g/2 oz butter
65 g/2½ oz plain flour, sifted
2 medium eggs, lightly beaten

For the custard:

300 ml/½ pint milk
pinch of freshly grated nutmeg
3 medium egg yolks
50 g/2 oz caster sugar
2 tbsp plain flour, sifted
2 tbsp cornflour, sifted

For the sauce:

175 g/6 oz soft brown sugar
150 ml/¼ pint boiling water
1 tsp instant coffee
1 tbsp cocoa powder
1 tbsp brandy
75 g/3 oz butter
1 tbsp golden syrup)

1 Preheat the oven to 220°C/425°F/Gas Mark 7, 15 minutes before cooking. Lightly oil two baking sheets. For the pastry, place the water and the butter in a heavy-based saucepan and bring to the boil. Remove from the heat and beat in the flour. Return to the heat and cook for 1 minute or until the mixture forms a ball in the centre of the saucepan.

2 Remove from the heat and leave to cool slightly, then gradually beat in the eggs a little at a time, beating well after each addition. Once all the eggs have been added, beat until the paste is smooth and glossy. Pipe or spoon 20 small balls onto the baking sheets, allowing plenty of room for expansion.

3 Bake in the preheated oven for 25 minutes or until well risen and golden brown. Reduce the oven temperature to 180°C/350°F/Gas Mark 4. Make a hole in each ball and continue to bake for a further 5 minutes. Remove from the oven and leave to cool.

4 For the custard, place the milk and nutmeg in a heavy-based saucepan and bring to the boil. In another saucepan, whisk together the egg yolks, sugar and the flours, then beat in the hot milk. Bring to the boil and simmer, whisking constantly for 2 minutes. Cover and leave to cool.

5 Spoon the custard into the profiteroles and arrange on a large serving dish. Place all the sauce ingredients in a small saucepan and bring to the boil, then simmer for 10 minutes. Remove from the heat and cool slightly before serving with the chocolate profiteroles.

1

2

5

Iced Chocolate & Raspberry Mousse

INGREDIENTS

Serves 4

12 sponge finger biscuits
juice of 2 oranges
2 tbsp Grand Marnier
300 ml/¹/₂ pint double cream
175 g/6 oz plain dark chocolate,
  broken into small pieces
225 g/8 oz frozen raspberries
6 tbsp icing sugar, sifted
cocoa powder, for dusting

To decorate:

few fresh whole raspberries
few mint leaves
grated white chocolate

1 Break the sponge finger biscuits into small pieces and divide between four individual glass dishes. Blend together the orange juice and Grand Marnier, then drizzle evenly over the sponge fingers. Cover with clingfilm and chill in the refrigerator for 30 minutes.

2 Meanwhile, place the cream in a small heavy-based saucepan and heat gently, stirring occasionally until boiling. Remove the saucepan from the heat then add the pieces of dark chocolate and leave to stand, untouched for about 7 minutes. Using a whisk, whisk the chocolate and cream together, until the chocolate has melted and is well blended and completely smooth. Leave to cool slightly.

3 Place the frozen raspberries and icing sugar into a food processor or liquidizer and blend until roughly crushed.

4 Fold the crushed raspberries into the cream and chocolate mixture and mix lightly until well blended. Spoon over the chilled sponge finger biscuits. Lightly dust with a little cocoa powder and decorate with whole raspberries, mint leaves and grated white chocolate. Serve immediately.

HELPFUL HINT

Remove the raspberries from the freezer about 20 minutes before you need to purée them. This will soften them slightly but they will still be frozen.

Chocolate Raspberry Mille Feuille

INGREDIENTS

Serves 6

450 g/1 lb puff pastry,
   thawed if frozen
1 quantity Raspberry Chocolate
   Ganache (see page 218), chilled
700 g/1½ lbs fresh raspberries, plus
   extra for decorating
icing sugar for dusting

For the raspberry sauce:

225 g/8 oz fresh raspberries
2 tbsp seedless raspberry jam
1–2 tbsp caster sugar, or to taste
2 tbsp lemon juice or
   framboise liqueur

HELPFUL HINT

If you prefer, make one big mille feuille by leaving the three strips whole in step 2. Slice the finished mille feuille with a sharp serrated knife.

1 Preheat the oven to 200°C/400°F/Gas Mark 6, 15 minutes before baking. Lightly oil a large baking sheet and sprinkle with a little water. Roll out the pastry on a lightly floured surface to a rectangle about 43 x 28 cm/17 x 11 inches. Cut into three long strips. Mark each strip crossways at 6.5 cm/2 ½ inch intervals using a sharp knife; this will make cutting the baked pastry easier and neater. Carefully transfer to the baking sheet, keeping the edges as straight as possible.

2 Bake in the preheated oven for 20 minutes or until well risen and golden brown. Place on a wire rack and leave to cool. Carefully transfer each rectangle to a work surface and using a sharp knife, trim the long edges straight. Cut along the knife marks to make 18 rectangles.

3 Place all the ingredients for the raspberry sauce in a food processor and blend until smooth. If the purée is too thick, add a little water. Taste and adjust the sweetness if necessary. Strain into a bowl, cover and chill in the refrigerator.

4 Place one pastry rectangle on the work surface flat-side down, spread with a little chocolate ganache and sprinkle with a few fresh raspberries. Spread a second rectangle with a little ganache, place over the first, pressing gently, then sprinkle with a few raspberries. Place a third rectangle on top, flat-side up, and spread with a little chocolate ganache.

5 Arrange some raspberries on top and dust lightly with a little icing sugar. Repeat with the remaining pastry rectangles, chocolate ganache and fresh raspberries.

6 Chill in the refrigerator until required and serve with the raspberry sauce and any remaining fresh raspberries.

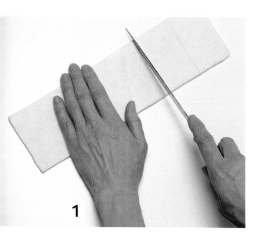

1

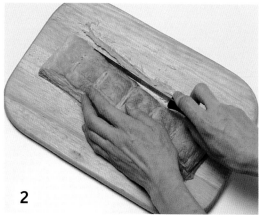

2

5

Vanilla & Lemon Panna Cotta with Raspberry Sauce

INGREDIENTS

Serves 6

900 ml/1½ pints double cream

1 vanilla pod, split

100 g/3½ oz caster sugar

zest of 1 lemon

3 sheets gelatine

5 tbsp milk

450 g/1 lb raspberries

3–4 tbsp icing sugar, to taste

1 tbsp lemon juice

extra lemon zest, to decorate

1. Put the cream, vanilla pod and sugar into a saucepan. Bring to the boil, then simmer for 10 minutes until slightly reduced, stirring to prevent scalding. Remove from the heat, stir in the lemon zest and remove the vanilla pod.

2. Soak the gelatine in the milk for 5 minutes, or until softened. Squeeze out any excess milk and add to the hot cream. Stir well until dissolved.

3. Pour the cream mixture into six ramekins or mini pudding moulds and leave in the refrigerator for 4 hours, or until set.

4. Meanwhile, put 175 g/6 oz of the raspberries in a food processor with the icing sugar and lemon juice. Blend to a purée then pass the mixture through a sieve. Fold in the remaining raspberries with a metal spoon or rubber spatula and chill in the refrigerator until ready to serve.

5. To serve, dip each of the moulds into hot water for a few seconds, then turn out on to six individual serving plates. Spoon some of the raspberry sauce over and around the panna cotta, decorate with extra lemon zest and serve.

TASTY TIP

Sheet gelatine is readily available from large supermarkets. It is much easier to measure and use than powdered gelatine and also gives a glossier finish to clear jellies.

1

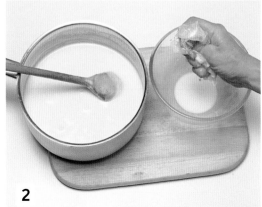
2

4

Bomba Siciliana

INGREDIENTS

Serves 6-8

100 g/3½ oz plain chocolate, broken
  into pieces
200 g/7 oz fresh chilled custard
150 ml/¼ pint whipping cream
25 g/1 oz candied peel,
  finely chopped
25 g/1 oz glacé cherries, chopped
25 g/1 oz sultanas
3 tbsp rum
225 g/8 oz good-quality vanilla
  ice cream
200 ml/¼ pint double cream
3 tbsp caster sugar

TASTY TIP

For the best flavour, buy whole candied peel. Cut it into strips using kitchen scissors, then chop crosswise into small pieces.

1   Melt the plain chocolate in bowl set over a saucepan of simmering water until smooth, then cool. Whisk together the custard with the whipping cream and slightly cooled chocolate Spoon the mixture into a shallow, lidded freezer box and freeze. Every 2 hours, remove from the freezer and using an electric whisk or balloon whisk, whisk thoroughly. Repeat 3 times, then leave until frozen solid. Soak the candied peel, cherries and sultanas in the rum and leave until needed.

2   Chill a bombe or 1 litre/1¾ pint pudding mould in the freezer for about 30 minutes. Remove the chocolate ice cream from the freezer to soften, then spoon the ice cream into the mould and press down well, smoothing around the edges and leaving a hollow in the centre. Return the ice cream to the freezer for about 1 hour, or until frozen hard.

3   Remove the vanilla ice cream from the freezer to soften. Spoon the softened vanilla ice cream into the hollow, making sure to leave another hollow for the cream. Return to the freezer again and freeze until hard.

4   Whip the cream and sugar until it is just holding its shape then fold in the soaked fruit. Remove the mould from the freezer and spoon in the cream mixture. Return to the freezer for at least another hour.

5   When ready to serve, remove the mould from the freezer and dip into hot water for a few seconds, then turn on to a large serving plate. Dip a knife into hot water and cut into wedges to serve.

1

1   2

Summer Fruit Semifreddo

INGREDIENTS

Serves 6-8

225 g/8 oz raspberries
125 g/4 oz blueberries
125 g/4 oz redcurrants
50 g/2 oz icing sugar
juice of 1 lemon
1 vanilla pod, split
50 g/2 oz sugar
4 large eggs, separated
600 ml/1 pint double cream
pinch of salt
fresh redcurrants, to decorate

1 Wash and hull or remove stalks from the fruits, as necessary, then put them into a food processor or blender with the icing sugar and lemon juice. Blend to a purée, pour into a jug and chill in the refrigerator, until needed.

2 Remove the seeds from the vanilla pod by opening the pod and scraping with the back of a knife. Add the seeds to the sugar and whisk with the egg yolks until pale and thick.

3 In another bowl, whip the cream until soft peaks form. Do not overwhip. In a third bowl, whip the egg whites with the salt until stiff peaks form.

4 Using a large metal spoon – to avoid knocking any air from the mixture – fold together the fruit purée, egg yolk mixture, the cream and egg whites. Transfer the mixture to a round, shallow, lidded freezer box and put into the freezer until almost frozen. If the mixture freezes solid, thaw in the refrigerator until semi-frozen. Turn out the semi-frozen mixture, cut into wedges and serve decorated with a few fresh redcurrants. If the mixture thaws completely, eat immediately and do not refreeze.

TASTY TIP

Use the egg and cream mixture as the basis for a host of other flavours, such as praline, chocolate, or autumn berries.

1

2

4

Frozen Amaretti Soufflé with Strawberries

INGREDIENTS

Serves 6–8

125 g/4 oz Amaretti biscuits
9 tbsp Amaretto liqueur
grated zest and juice of 1 lemon
1 tbsp powdered gelatine
6 medium eggs, separated
175 g/6 oz soft brown sugar
600 ml/1 pint double cream
450 g/1 lb fresh strawberries,
   halved if large
1 vanilla pod, split and seeds
   scraped out
2 tbsp caster sugar
few finely crushed Amaretti biscuits,
   to decorate

HELPFUL HINT

When making ice cream it is important to set the freezer to rapid freeze at least 2 hours beforehand. Remember to return the freezer to its normal setting when you have finished.

1 Wrap a collar of greaseproof paper around a 900 ml/1½ pint soufflé dish or six to eight individual ramekin dishes to extend at least 5 cm/2 inch above the rim and secure with string. Break the Amaretti biscuits into a bowl. Sprinkle over 6 tablespoons of the Amaretto liqueur and leave to soak.

2 Put the lemon zest and juice into a small heatproof bowl and sprinkle over the gelatine. Leave for 5 minutes to sponge, then put the bowl over a saucepan of simmering water, ensuring that the base of the bowl does not touch the water. Stir occasionally until the gelatine has dissolved completely.

3 In a clean bowl, whisk the egg yolks and sugar until pale and thick then stir in the gelatine and the soaked biscuits. In another bowl, lightly whip 450 ml/¾ pint of the cream and using a large metal spoon or rubber spatula fold into the mixture. In a third clean bowl, whisk the egg whites until stiff, then fold into the soufflé mixture. Transfer to the prepared dish, or individual ramekin dishes, and level the top. Freeze for at least 8 hours, or preferably overnight.

4 Put the strawberries into a bowl with the vanilla pod and seeds, sugar and remaining Amaretto liqueur. Leave overnight in the refrigerator, then allow to come to room temperature before serving.

5 Place the soufflé in the refrigerator for about 1 hour. Whip the remaining cream and use to decorate the soufflé then sprinkle a few finely crushed Amaretti biscuits on the top and serve with the strawberries.

1

2

3

Zabaglione with Rum–soaked Raisin Compote

INGREDIENTS

Serves 6

2 tbsp raisins

1 strip thinly pared lemon zest

½ tsp ground cinnamon

3 tbsp Marsala wine

3 medium egg yolks

3 tbsp caster sugar

125 ml/4 fl oz dry white wine

150 ml/¼ pint double cream,
  lightly whipped

crisp biscuits, to serve

FOOD FACT

Zabaglione, an Italian concoction of eggs, sugar and wine is virtually identical to Sabayon – a French concoction of eggs, sugar and wine. Make the zabaglione as above and omit the raisins. Serve with poached pears, summer fruits or on its own in stemmed glasses.

1 Put the raisins in a small bowl with the lemon zest and ground cinnamon. Pour over the Marsala wine to cover and leave to macerate for at least one hour. When the raisins are plump, lift out of the Marsala wine and reserve the raisins and wine, discarding the lemon zest.

2 In a large heatproof bowl, mix together the egg yolks and sugar. Add the white wine and Marsala wine and stir well to combine. Put the bowl over a saucepan of simmering water, ensuring that the bottom of the bowl does not touch the water. Whisk constantly until the mixture doubles in bulk.

3 Remove from the heat and continue whisking for about 5 minutes until the mixture has cooled slightly. Fold in the raisins and then immediately fold in the whipped cream. Spoon into dessert glasses or goblets and serve with crisp biscuits.

1

2

3

Tiramisu

INGREDIENTS

Serves 4

225 g/8 oz mascarpone cheese
25 g/1 oz icing sugar, sifted
150 ml/¼ pint strong brewed
  coffee, chilled
300 ml/½ pint double cream
3 tbsp coffee liqueur
125 g/4 oz Savoiardi or
  sponge finger biscuits
50 g/2 oz plain dark chocolate, grated
  or made into small curls
cocoa powder, for dusting
assorted summer berries, to serve

1 Lightly oil and line a 900 g/2 lb loaf tin with a piece of clingfilm. Put the mascarpone cheese and icing sugar into a large bowl and using a rubber spatula, beat until smooth. Stir in 2 tablespoons of chilled coffee and mix thoroughly.

2 Whip the cream with 1 tablespoon of the coffee liqueur until just thickened. Stir a spoonful of the whipped cream into the mascarpone mixture, then fold in the rest. Spoon half of the the mascarpone mixture into the prepared loaf tin and smooth the top.

3 Put the remaining coffee and coffee liqueur into a shallow dish just bigger than the biscuits. Using half of the biscuits, dip one side of each biscuit into the coffee mixture, then arrange on top of the mascarpone mixture in a single layer. Spoon the rest of the mascarpone mixture over the biscuits and smooth the top.

4 Dip the remaining biscuits in the coffee mixture and arrange on top of the mascarpone mixture. Drizzle with any remaining coffee mixture. Cover with clingfilm and chill in the refrigerator for 4 hours.

5 Carefully turn the tiramisu out on to a large serving plate and sprinkle with the grated chocolate or chocolate curls. Dust with cocoa powder, cut into slices and serve with a few summer berries.

FOOD FACT

This now classic Italian dessert appears in all kinds of forms in most Italian cookery books. The name literally means 'pick me up'.

1

2

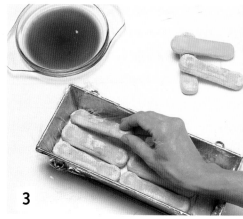

3

Chocolate & Rum Truffles

INGREDIENTS

Makes 44

For the chocolate truffles:

225 g/8 oz plain chocolate
25 g/1 oz butter, softened
2 medium egg yolks
2 tsp brandy or kirsch
2 tsp double cream
24 maraschino cherries, drained
2 tbsp cocoa powder, sifted

For the rum truffles:

125 g/4 oz plain dark chocolate
2 tbsp rum
125 ml/4 fl oz double cream
50 g/2 oz ground almonds
2 tbsp icing sugar, sifted

TASTY TIP

These truffles are so easy to make, they are great to give as gifts. Roll some in icing sugar, as above, and roll others in cocoa powder. Arrange in a gift box in a chequerboard pattern.

1 For the chocolate truffles, break the chocolate into pieces and place in a heatproof bowl set over a saucepan of gently simmering water. Leave for 20 minutes or until the chocolate has melted. Stir until the chocolate is smooth and remove from the heat. Leave to stand for about 6 minutes.

2 Beat the butter, the egg yolks, the brandy or kirsch and double cream together until smooth. Stir the melted chocolate into the butter and egg yolk mixture and stir until thick. Cover and leave to cool for about 30 minutes. Chill in the refrigerator for 1 ½ hours or until firm.

3 Divide the truffle mixture into 24 pieces and mould around the drained cherries. Roll in the cocoa powder until evenly coated. Place the truffles in petit four paper cases and chill in the refrigerator for 2 hours before serving.

4 To make the rum truffles, break the chocolate into small pieces and place in a heavy-based saucepan with the cream and rum. Heat gently until the chocolate has melted, then stir until smooth. Stir in the ground almonds and pour into a small bowl and chill in the refrigerator for at least 6 hours or until the mixture is thick.

5 Remove the truffle from the refrigerator and shape small spoonfuls, about the size of a cherry, into balls. Roll in the sifted icing sugar and place in petit four paper cases. Store the truffles in the refrigerator until ready to serve.

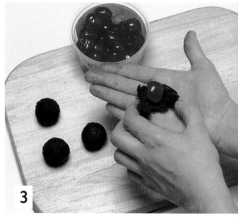

Shortbread Thumbs

INGREDIENTS

Makes 12

125 g/4 oz self-raising flour
125 g/4 oz butter, softened
25 g/1 oz white vegetable fat
50 g/2 oz granulated sugar
25 g/1 oz cornflour, sifted
5 tbsp cocoa powder, sifted
125 g/4 oz icing sugar
6 assorted coloured glacé cherries,
   rinsed, dried and halved

FOOD FACT

Using a combination of butter and vegetable fat gives these biscuits a softer texture than using all butter.

HELPFUL HINT

After baking, remove the cooked biscuits as soon as possible from the baking sheets as they will continue to cook and could overcook. Cool completely on wire cooling racks before storing in airtight tins.

1   Preheat the oven to 150°C/300°F/Gas Mark 2, 10 minutes before baking. Lightly oil two baking sheets. Sift the flour into a large bowl, cut 75 g/3 oz of the butter and the white vegetable fat into small cubes, add to the flour, then, using your fingertips, rub in until the mixture resembles fine breadcrumbs.

2   Stir in the granulated sugar, sifted cornflour and 4 tablespoons of cocoa powder and bring the mixture together with your hand to form a soft and pliable dough.

3   Place on a lightly floured surface and shape into 12 small balls. Place onto the baking sheets at least 5 cm/2 inches apart, then press each one with a clean thumb to make a dent.

4   Bake in the preheated oven for 20–25 minutes. Remove from the oven and leave for 1–2 minutes to cool. Transfer to a wire rack and leave until cold.

5   Sift the icing sugar and the remaining cocoa powder into a bowl and add the remaining softened butter. Blend to form a smooth and spreadable icing with 1–2 tablespoons of hot water. Spread a little icing over the top of each biscuit and place half a cherry on each. Leave until set before serving.

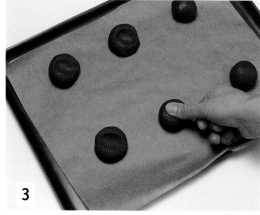

Chocolate Orange Biscuits

INGREDIENTS

Makes 30

100 g/3 ½ oz plain dark chocolate
125 g/4 oz butter
125 g/4 oz caster sugar
pinch of salt
1 medium egg, beaten
grated zest of 2 oranges
200 g/7 oz plain flour
1 tsp baking powder
125 g/4 oz icing sugar
1–2 tbsp orange juice

HELPFUL HINT

To get the maximum amount of juice from citrus fruits, heat the whole fruit in the microwave for about 40 seconds, then cool slightly before squeezing. alternatively, roll the fruit on the table, pressing lightly before squeezing out the juice. It is important to add the orange juice gradually to the icing mixture because you may not need all of it to obtain a spreadable consistency.

1 Preheat the oven to 200°C/400°F/Gas Mark 6, 15 minutes before baking. Lightly oil several baking sheets. Coarsely grate the chocolate and reserve. Beat the butter and sugar together until creamy. Add the salt, beaten egg and half the orange zest and beat again.

2 Sift the flour and baking powder, add to the bowl with the grated chocolate and beat to form a dough. Shape into a ball, wrap in clingfilm and chill in the refrigerator for 2 hours.

3 Roll the dough out on a lightly floured surface to 5 mm/¼ inch thickness and cut into 5 cm/2 inch rounds. Place the rounds on the prepared baking sheets, allowing room for expansion. Bake in the preheated oven for 10–12 minutes or until firm. Remove the biscuits from the oven and leave to cool slightly. Using a spatula, transfer to a wire rack and leave to cool.

4 Sift the icing sugar into a small bowl and stir in sufficient orange juice to make a smooth, spreadable icing. Pipe spirals of icing on to the biscuits, leave until almost set, then sprinkle on the remaining grated orange zest before serving.

1

2

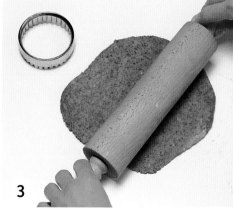
3

Rich Chocolate Cup Cakes

INGREDIENTS

Makes 12

175 g/6 oz self-raising flour
25 g/1 oz cocoa powder
175 g/6 oz soft light brown sugar
75 g/3 oz butter, melted
2 medium eggs, lightly beaten
1 tsp vanilla essence
40 g/1½ oz maraschino cherries,
   drained and chopped

For the chocolate icing:

50 g/2 oz plain dark chocolate
25 g/1 oz unsalted butter
25 g/1 oz icing sugar, sifted

For the cherry icing:

125 g/4 oz icing sugar
7 g/¼ oz unsalted butter, melted
1 tsp syrup from the
   maraschino cherries
3 maraschino cherries, halved,
   to decorate

1 Preheat the oven to 180°C/350°F/Gas Mark 4, 10 minutes before baking. Line a 12 hole muffin or deep bun tin tray with paper muffin cases. Sift the flour and cocoa powder into a bowl. Stir in the sugar, then add the melted butter, eggs and vanilla essence. Beat together with a wooden spoon for 3 minutes or until well blended.

2 Divide half the mixture between six of the paper cases. Dry the cherries thoroughly on absorbent kitchen paper, then fold into the remaining mixture and spoon into the rest of the paper cases.

3 Bake on the shelf above the centre of the preheated oven for 20 minutes, or until a skewer inserted into the centre of a cake comes out clean. Transfer to a wire rack and leave to cool.

4 For the chocolate icing, melt the chocolate and butter in a heatproof bowl set over a saucepan of hot water. Remove from the heat and leave to cool for 3 minutes, stirring occasionally. Stir in the icing sugar. Spoon over the six plain chocolate cakes and leave to set.

5 For the cherry icing, sift the icing sugar into a bowl and stir in 1 tablespoon of boiling water, the butter and cherry syrup. Spoon the icing over the remaining six cakes, decorate each with a halved cherry and leave to set.

1

3

4

Chocolate Fudge Brownies

INGREDIENTS

Makes 16

125 g/4 oz butter

175 g/6 oz plain dark chocolate, roughly chopped or broken

225 g/8 oz caster sugar

2 tsp vanilla essence

2 medium eggs, lightly beaten

150 g/5 oz plain flour

175 g/6 oz icing sugar

2 tbsp cocoa powder

15 g/½ oz butter

FOOD FACT

Chocolate is obtained from the bean of the cacao tree and was introduced to Europe in the 16th Century. It is available in many different forms from cocoa powder to couverture, which is the best chocolate to use for cooking as it has a high cocoa butter content and melts very smoothly.

1 Preheat the oven to 180°C/350°F/Gas Mark 4 10 minutes before baking. Lightly oil and line a 20.5 cm/8 inch square cake tin with greaseproof or baking paper.

2 Slowly melt the butter and chocolate together in a heatproof bowl set over a sauce-pan of simmering water. Transfer the mixture to a large bowl.

3 Stir in the sugar and vanilla essence, then stir in the eggs. Sift over the flour and fold together well with a metal spoon or rubber spatula. Pour into the prepared tin.

4 Transfer to the preheated oven and bake for 30 minutes until just set. Remove the cooked mixture from the oven and leave to cool in the tin before turning it out on to a wire rack.

5 Sift the icing sugar and cocoa powder into a small bowl and make a well in the centre.

6 Place the butter in the well then gradually add about 2 tablespoons of hot water. Mix to form a smooth spreadable icing.

7 Pour the icing over the cooked mixture. Allow the icing to set before cutting into squares. Serve the brownies when they are cold.

2

3

5

Jammy Buns

INGREDIENTS

Makes 12

175 g/6 oz plain flour
175 g/6 oz wholemeal flour
2 tsp baking powder
150 g/5 oz butter or margarine
125 g/4 oz golden caster sugar
50 g/2 oz dried cranberries
1 large egg, beaten
1 tbsp milk
4–5 tbsp seedless raspberry jam

TASTY TIP

In this recipe any type of jam can be used. However, look for one with a high-fruit content. Alternatively replace the jam with a fruit compote. Simply boil some fruit with a little sugar and water, then leave to cool before placing inside the buns.

1. Preheat the oven to 190°C/375°F/Gas Mark 5, 10 minutes before baking. Lightly oil a large baking sheet.

2. Sift the flours and baking powder together into a large bowl, then tip in the grains remaining in the sieve.

3. Cut the butter or margarine into small pieces. (It is easier to do this when the butter is in the flour as it helps stop the butter from sticking to the knife.)

4. Rub the butter into the flours until it resembles coarse breadcrumbs. Stir in the sugar and cranberries.

5. Using a round bladed knife stir in the beaten egg and milk. Mix to form a firm dough. Divide the mixture into 12 and roll into balls.

6. Place the dough balls on the baking tray, leaving enough space for expansion. Press the thumb into the centre of each ball making a small hollow.

7. Spoon a little of the jam in each hollow and bake in the preheated oven for 20–25 minutes, or until golden brown. Cool on a wire rack and serve.

4

6

7

Whisked Sponge Cake

INGREDIENTS

Cuts into 6 slices

125 g/4 oz plain flour, plus 1 tsp
175 g/6 oz caster sugar, plus 1 tsp
3 medium eggs
1 tsp vanilla essence
4 tbsp raspberry jam
50 g/2 oz fresh raspberries, crushed
icing sugar, to dredge

TASTY TIP

For a creamier low-fat filling mix the crushed raspberries or strawberries with 4 tablespoons each of low-fat Greek yogurt and low-fat crème fraîche.

1 Preheat the oven to 200°C/400°F/Gas Mark 6 15 minutes before baking. Mix 1 teaspoon of the flour and 1 teaspoon of the sugar together. Lightly oil two 18 cm/7 inch sandwich tins and dust lightly with the sugar and flour.

2 Place the eggs in a large heatproof bowl. Add the sugar, then place over a saucepan of gently simmering water ensuring that the base of the bowl does not touch the hot water. Using an electric whisk beat the sugar and eggs until they become light and fluffy. (The whisk should leave a trail in the mixture when it is lifted out.)

3 Remove the bowl from the saucepan of water, add the vanilla essence and continue beating for 2–3 minutes. Sift the flour gently into the egg mixture and using a metal spoon or rubber spatula carefully fold in, taking care not to over mix and remove all the air that has been whisked in.

4 Divide the mixture between the two prepared cake tins. Tap lightly on the work surface to remove any air bubbles. Bake in the preheated oven for 20–25 minutes, or until golden. Test that the cake is ready by gently pressing the centre with a clean finger – it should spring back.

5 Leave to cool in the tins for 5 minutes, then turn out on to a wire rack. Blend the jam and the crushed raspberries together. When the cakes are cold spread over the jam mixture and sandwich together. Dredge the top with icing sugar and serve.

1

2

5

Chocolate Fudge Sundae

INGREDIENTS

Serves 2

For the chocolate fudge sauce:

75 g/3 oz plain dark chocolate, broken into pieces

450ml/³/₄ pint double cream

175g/6 oz golden caster sugar

25 g/1 oz plain flour

pinch of salt

15 g/¹/₂ oz unsalted butter

1 tsp vanilla essence

For the sundae:

125 g/4 oz raspberries, fresh or thawed if frozen

3 scoops vanilla ice cream

2 scoops chocolate ice cream

2 tbsp toasted flaked almonds

a few wafers, to serve

1. To make the chocolate fudge sauce, place the chocolate and cream in a heavy-based saucepan and heat gently until the chocolate has melted into the cream. Stir until smooth. Mix the sugar with the flour and salt, then stir in sufficient chocolate mixture to make a smooth paste.

2. Gradually blend the remaining melted chocolate mixture into the paste, then pour into a clean saucepan. Cook over a low heat, stirring frequently until smooth and thick. Remove from the heat and add the butter and vanilla essence. Stir until smooth, then cool slightly.

3. To make the sundae, crush the raspberries lightly with a fork and reserve. Spoon a little of the chocolate sauce into the bottom of two sundae glasses. Add a layer of crushed raspberries, then a scoop each of vanilla and chocolate ice cream.

4. Top each one with a scoop of the vanilla ice cream. Pour over the sauce, sprinkle over the almonds and serve with a wafer.

2

3

3

Index